Fifty Hikes in West Virginia

Fifty Hikes in West Virginia

Short Walks, Day Hikes, and Overnights
in the Mountain State and
Western Maryland

ANN and JIM McGRAW

Photographs by the authors

Backcountry Publications
Woodstock,
Vermont

An Invitation to the Reader

Over time trails can be rerouted and signs and landmarks altered. If you find that changes have occurred on the routes described in this book, please let us know so that corrections may be made in future editions. The author and publisher also welcome other comments and suggestions. Address all correspondence to:

Editor, Fifty Hikes
Backcountry Publications
P.O. Box 175
Woodstock, VT 05091

Library of Congress Cataloging-in-Publication Data

McGraw, Ann, 1954–
   Fifty hikes in West Virginia.

   Bibliography: p.
   1. Hiking—West Virginia—Guide-books.   2. West
Virginia—Description and travel—Guide-books.
I. McGraw, Jim, 1956–   II. Title.
GV199.42.W4M34 1986   917.54'0443   86-7849
ISBN 0-942440-32-3

Published by Backcountry Publications, Inc.
Woodstock, Vermont 05091

Printed in the United States of America

Text and cover design by Wladislaw Finne
Trail overlays by Richard Widhu

To Ian and Trevor

Contents

Introduction 9

Northern Hills Province

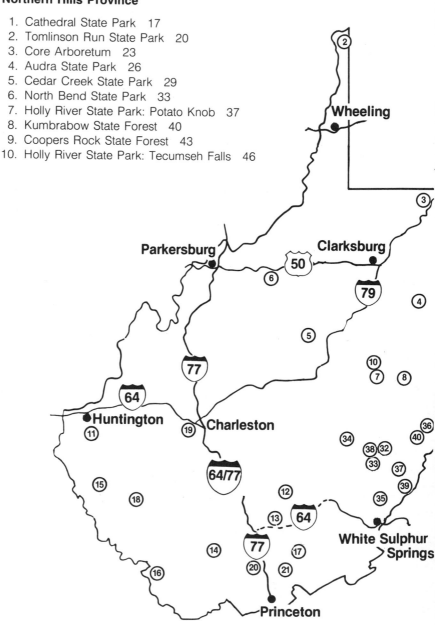

Southern Hills Province

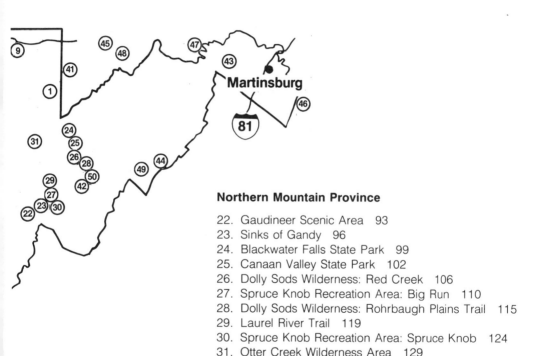

Northern Mountain Province

Southern Mountain Province

Ridge and Valley Province

Introduction

West Virginia is a state that conjures up strong images. To many non-natives, West Virginia means coal mining, poverty, and isolation from modern civilization: a sort of vast no-man's land between the bustling eastern seaboard and the fertile midwest. For travelers passing through, West Virginia means slow going; the terrain is rugged and hilly. But to many West Virginians, and to a growing number of others, the state is also one of great natural beauty. To these people, it is the "wild, wonderful" West Virginia that earns a special place in their hearts. This book is an invitation to discover firsthand the beauty of the land appropriately known as "almost heaven."

West Virginia can be divided roughly into three physiographic provinces. In the northeastern part of the state is the "ridge and valley" province, which is characterized by long parallel ridges with wide fertile valleys between them. Here are the largest areas of flat land in the state, so the area seems tame when compared with the rest.

The tallest mountains lie just to the west in an area known as the Allegheny Mountain province. The mountains are high by eastern standards, with many peaks rising above 4,000 feet. Summits, though, are often just high points on a long ridge, and the high valleys between the ridges make the mountains seem smaller than they really are. Nevertheless, with their more northerly climate and vegetation, the highlands have a special appeal in any season. On hot mid-summer days you can escape to the cool breezes and clear rushing streams of the mountains. In fall, the foliage displays in the northern hardwood forests at high elevations can rival any New England scene. In winter, deep snows here transform the landscape once more. In spring and early summer, the forest wildflowers reach their peak and the woods are filled with birds following their annual migration routes.

As you go west, the mountains grade into the Allegheny Plateau or hills province, which accounts for the greatest land area in West Virginia. In any one area within the hills province, the tops of the hills all lie at about the same elevation. The valleys or "hollows" between hilltops were formed by the erosion of a flat plateau (hence the name Allegheny Plateau, despite the steep terrain). In much of the state, the steep hills are cloaked by second-growth mixed hardwood forest with a rich understory of beautiful wildflowers.

The climate of West Virginia falls within the general range typical of temperate zones, with pronounced seasons and precipitation distributed throughout the year. Despite the small size of the state, West Virginia's climate is surprisingly variable. This variation is due in part to the northern and eastern reach of the state's two panhandles. Elevation also influences the regional climate through its effect on temperature and hence growing season length. The west-to-east movement of air across the mountains squeezes moisture from the air on the west side, leaving the far eastern part of the state comparatively dry.

West Virginia's vegetation is largely eastern deciduous forest, but here too variability is the rule. There are dry oak-pine forests in the east, northern or Allegheny hardwoods in the mountains, and mixed hardwoods at lower elevations. Even within these categories, there are variations. For example, steep slopes and bottom lands support different complements of hardwood tree species. Over limited areas, there are pockets of unique plant communities such as northern bogs, shale barrens, and heath barrens. The red spruce forests that once were widespread in the mountains have lost ground after lumbering and are limited now to a few of the highest ridges. The understory flora of the forests in some areas provides some of the finest spring wildflower shows anywhere in the east. Vast stands of trillium, Virginia bluebell, trout lily, jack-in-the-pulpit, bloodroot, mountain laurel, and great rhododendron, to name a few species, are common.

Wildlife is abundant in West Virginia's woods. Deer are encountered frequently, and signs of bear and bobcat are common. A few of West Virginia's "charismatic vertebrates," such as the elk and mountain lion, are now extinct, or nearly extinct, in the state, while others such as the beaver and raven have made dramatic comebacks from the brink of extinction in the last few decades. Animals such as the flying squirrel, opposum, and raccoon are common, yet they are rarely observed because of their nocturnal habits. Birds are some of the most visible wildlife in the forest, and West Virginia is noted for its warbler and hawk migrations. While native stream fish have suffered from water quality problems in many places, selected streams still support healthy fish populations. Trout and other game fish are stocked in many of the state's streams, rivers, and lakes.

Fortunately for hikers, West Virginia is blessed by a very low incidence of insect pests such as mosquitoes, deer flies, and black flies. Two poisonous snakes, the eastern timber rattler and the copperhead, occur in the state. Like most snakes, they are shy animals, and one rarely encounters them. Garter snakes and black racers, on the other hand, are commonly seen, but they are harmless.

Hikers new to West Virginia may be surprised and pleased to learn that most of the hiking trails are not overused, and yet some of the finest trails in the east are found here. Even on weekends and holidays, it is not unusual to have a trail to yourself. Along with solitude, you will find relatively unspoiled forests as you leave the roadside. Evidence abounds of man's past activities -- lumbering railroad grades (which often form the path), mining equipment, old farm fences, and apple trees -- but today West Virginia's woods are maturing, for the most part, undisturbed.

A few hours of walking in the woods, and the burdens of everyday life begin to fade away. In a stressful world, hiking provides a way to relax and to gain perspective. At the same time that your mind unwinds, your body benefits from one of the most effective types of cardiovascular workouts known to man -- simple walking. What's more, you get the exercise benefit of hiking with no specialized, expensive machinery and virtually no special clothing or accessories. By varying your pace or by following terrain of varying difficulty, you can fine-tune your hiking to the level of exercise you want to achieve. As the novelty of the current craze in rowing/biking/weightlifting machines for the living room begins to wear thin, more and more exercise-

Chipmunk

conscious and budget-minded people will discover, or rediscover, the ancient, time-proven exercise of walking.

About This Book
This book describes fifty selected hikes in West Virginia and the panhandle of western Maryland. We chose hikes to represent all the physiographic provinces, and within each province we attempted to find hikes to suit a range of hikers from young to old and from newcomers to seasoned veterans. Beyond these criteria, we tried to select hikes that made nice units, often combining several trails to make a circuit hike or to encompass side trips to points of interest.

Most of the hikes are entirely on public land -- in state parks, state forests, national forests, wilderness areas, recreation areas, or national historic parks. A few of them cross private land for short distances, but their inclusion in this book is not intended to imply that the landowners have given permission for anyone to cross their land. If you have any doubt about whether access is permissible, we urge you to call or write the landowner directly. A ranger can often tell you who to ask. Most landowners are kind enough to let hikers cross their land as long as gates are kept closed, the property remains undamaged, and refuse is packed out.

Distances along the trail were measured with a calibrated pedometer. This method works essentially by counting strides and is therefore subject to error if the hiker changes length of stride without changing the calibration. Hiking distances shown therefore should be viewed as approximate and not exact measurements. They are included primarily to indicate relative positions of trail junctions, points-of-interest, and landmarks along the way.

Hiking times are listed at the beginning of each hike. This will vary of course with the pace of each individual or group,

and the times given are intended only as a guideline. Novices (or birdwatchers and botanists!) will want to allow more time. Experienced hikers will have no difficulty bettering the times shown, but hiking is not a racing event: your pace should be whatever is comfortable for you.

The elevation change is the total cumulative vertical rise over the course of the hike, not the difference between elevation at trailhead and the highest point. This statistic gives you an idea of how much climbing is required along the route. In the frequently steep West Virginia terrain, this elevation change figure may be a better indicator of the difficulty of the hike than distance.

You can tell the most about a hike from a topographic map of the route. From a map you can determine approximate hike length and vertical rise, as well as gauge the steepness of the trail by the number of contour lines that are crossed per unit of distance. For each hike, a portion of a United States Geological Survey topographic map has been provided, which shows parking, trails, overlooks, and points-of-interest. The USGS quadrangle names are also given in case you want to purchase the entire quadrangle map yourself ($2.50 each for any quad in the state). We also list other maps that may be helpful, such as the park or forest maps that often are available.

Each hike description is preceded by a brief summary of highlights of the trail. There may be other highlights, of course, depending on your interests, the season of the year, and even the particular day of your hike. The same trail will provide different highlights for different people on the same day. Your lasting impression of a hike undoubtedly will be unique.

The Trails
We have divided the book into five sections. A range of hike lengths is found in

each section. Thirty hikes are suitable for morning or afternoon walks, ranging up to five miles in length. Sixteen hikes are classified as "day hikes," which are up to eleven miles in length. The four remaining hikes are best done as backpack trips and range up to twenty-seven miles long. Hike length does not always correspond to difficulty, though. The steepest trail of the lot is only 2.7 miles long (Seneca Rocks), while the longest is flat, easy walking for most of its length (North Fork Mountain).

Most of the trails we describe are well-worn footpaths. Some are well-marked with paint blazes, while others are marked only at junctions or not at all. Many of the trails cross mountain streams without bridges and require shallow wading. These streams can swell rapidly after a heavy downpour, making a crossing dangerous or impossible. Keep an eye on the weather on such hikes.

Trails in the Monongahela National Forest have been given identifying numbers as well as names. Often these numbers will be shown on the topographic maps with each hike. Frequently, signs at the trailhead and at trail junctions display the trail number. Because their use is somewhat sporadic, however, our trail descriptions do not rely on this numbering system.

Some of the hikes we describe are done most easily as shuttles with two vehicles. Any of them of course can be done by a single-car group by backtracking along the same route. Two of our hikes have options for riding a chairlift as part of the "hike." Purists can hike the entire way, however, and this route is described. One unusual hike follows a stream course underground through a long cave. The Greenbrier River Trail and Chesapeake and Ohio Canal Trail can be biked as well as hiked, providing yet another possibility for variety.

Equipment and Clothing
Undoubtedly the most important piece of equipment for hiking is footwear. Hiking guides used to be quite specific about the kind of shoes or boots to wear. We think this attitude is a bit outdated. The important features of good footwear are comfort and support. For some, this means sneakers; for others it means high-topped, steel-toed leather insulated boots; for most it means something in-between. One hiking friend actually prefers bare feet, although we don't recommend it for the average tenderfooted hiker. Novice hikers should try out different kinds of footwear on short hikes to discover their preference. This way a mistake in judgment won't be too costly in terms of sore feet.

As for clothing, common sense is all you need. You can spend hundreds of dollars on Gore-Tex parkas and raingear, but a basic raincoat and hat that successfully shed water will take care of bad weather in all but rare cases in warm seasons. Tight-weave long pants can be important on some of the less-traveled trails, for they can help protect against the nettles, blackberries, and dogbriar that often overgrow the trail. Layering of clothes is a good idea in the cool or cold seasons, so you can peel layers while you are walking, but replace them when you rest. If you hike, or ski, in winter you should be aware that the West Virginia climate is capable of temperatures well below zero for several days on end, particularly in the mountains. We suggest that you become thoroughly familiar with winter mountaineering before venturing far into the woods in winter.

For most of the hikes in this book, the only equipment you will need is a small knapsack to carry raingear, perhaps lunch or a snack, and water. Of course you will probably tote other favorite items such as binoculars, cameras, or field guides as well, but generally they can be packed into a small frameless knapsack.

For the four backpack trips described in this book, we recommend that you assemble a detailed equipment list by consulting one of the many excellent books devoted to backpacking that are widely available in bookstores and libraries.

We have purposely avoided commenting on the palatability of drinking water throughout our hike descriptions. We recommend that you carry enough liquids for the entire hike and avoid drinking from streams and rivers wherever possible. Water-purifying tablets will work if used correctly, and thorough boiling will sterilize water in an emergency. Too many of the small, wild-looking hollows have been subjected to human use and abuse in the past to let anyone make easy judgments about the safety of the drinking water. If you come across a clear, cold spring high in the mountains, probably it is safe and clean. Otherwise, it's best to assume that the water is not good to drink.

Hiking Etiquette

Common sense applies to good manners in the woods as well as to clothing. After twenty years of recent environmental conciousness, you might think that the admonition, "if you pack it in, pack it out," would be everyday knowledge. Judging by the condition of most West Virginia trails, the vast majority of hikers respect this first principle of good etiquette. Unfortunately, it takes only the occasional misinformed or thoughtless person to destroy the pristine quality of an area. As the managers of our public lands are rarely well-funded enough to clean up trash on hiking trails, we might add "and pack out more than you packed in" to the first principle of good etiquette.

A second tenet of good outdoor manners is basically the principle of sound conservation: Leave the woods as you found them. The flowers, animals, trees, and streams are there to be enjoyed, and they are there not only for you but for others as well. The conservation principle is often summed up as "take only pictures and leave only footprints."

Other Books

Hiking Guide to Monongahela National Forest and Vicinity
West Virginia Highlands Conservancy, 1983.

Hiking Guide to the Allegheny Trail
West Virginia Scenic Trails Association, 1983.
Post Office Box 4042
Charleston, WV 25304

Hiking Trails in the Southern Mountains
Jerry Sullivan and Glenda McDaniel
Chicago: Greatlakes Living Press, 1975.

Hiking Guide for the Big Schloss-Wolf Gap Area
Helen McGinnis.
Available from: Bill Dzombak
621 Spring Street
Latrobe, PA 15650

A Walker's Guide to Harper's Ferry, West Virginia
Dave Gilbert
Charleston: Pictorial Histories Publishing Company, 1983

Addresses for further information and maps

United States Forest Service
P. O. Box 1548
Elkins, West Virginia 26554

West Virginia Department of Commerce
State Capital Complex
Charleston, West Virginia 25305

Division of Parks and Recreation
Department of Natural Resources
Charleston, West Virginia 25305

Northern Hills Province

1

Cathedral State Park

Distance: 1.2 miles
Time: 3/4 hour
Elevation change: 80 feet
Maps: USGS 7½' Aurora, Park map
Highlight: Virgin hemlock forest

Cathedral State Park is home to one of the few remaining virgin stands of hemlock in West Virginia or anywhere in the East. Cathedral is centered around US 50, which was the major artery between Ohio and the East before the Baltimore and Ohio Railroad was completed. In its heyday, a continuous flow of stage coaches, carriages, horseback riders, and pedestrians streamed along this road through the hemlock forest. Probably many enjoyed their lunches beside the stream beneath the giant trees.

In addition, summer vacationers were drawn to the cool Appalachians to escape the city swelter. Near the present entrance of the park, Judge Vail of Harpers Ferry built the rambling Brookside Hotel in 1884 to cater to vacationers. Lee McBride, president of a prosperous Cleveland firm, and his wife fell in love with the area and built a large home opposite the hotel. In 1900, the McBrides bought Brookside Hotel and made it a popular summer resort. Even though between 1890 and 1910, gigantic logging companies were removing virgin timber from the surrounding hillside, the Cathedral forests were not denuded because they were essential to the hotel

Trail through a virgin forest

business for hiking, bridle paths, picnicking, and general aesthetic reasons.

In 1909, McBride died, and one of his workmen, Branson Haas, took over the place. He continued to protect the forest until 1942 when he sold the forest tract to the West Virginia Conservation Commission with the proviso that the forest "remain unexploited and [be] given every protection possible". Through the stewardship of these thoughtful owners, the stand in Cathedral State Park was preserved in its natural state. Since 1966, Cathedral State Park has been listed in the National Registry of Natural Historic Landmarks in recognition of its special character.

Cathedral State Park is accessible from US 50 at Aurora, north of the Monongahela National Forest. Park your car in the second parking lot (there are only two), which is about a hundred yards west of the park headquarters. The largest hemlock tree in West Virginia—the "centennial" hemlock—is located directly behind the park headquarters, and it is worth the short walk to see.

The hiking trail we describe begins in the second parking lot. The trail is short and level and therefore may be enjoyed by hikers of nearly any ability. It begins on the lower side of the lot at a wooden walkway that leads to a small wooden bridge over a creek. On the far side of the bridge, the trail forks. The right fork leads to a picnic area and playground. Follow the left fork. The trail immediately brings you to a cool, shady hemlock forest. Another fork is reached shortly after the first, and you go left again. The trail divides yet a third time, and you once again follow the left fork, staying close to US 50. Here there is a dense understory of rhododendron and laurel with ferns, trillium, wood sorrel, and other small plants at ground level. A fourth intersection is quickly reached, which may be the most confusing, as the Cathedral Trail you are following is not well-marked. Five paths converge here and you follow the third path, counting from the left. Cathedral Trail continues to parallel US 50.

In the next few hundred feet, you may notice that although the forest has not been directly altered by man, this does not mean that the forest is stable and unchanging on a small scale. Where large

hemlocks have died or been toppled by the wind, there are large gaps in the forest canopy where their crowns once were. Whether the entire forest is changing over the long term is difficult to observe directly, because such changes would occur on a time scale spanning several human lifetimes. The future of such a natural forest depends on which species of trees can most effectively invade the gaps created by the demise of individual hemlocks that we can see here.

You encounter yet another fork in the trail a few hundred feet beyond the last. Take the left fork again. At the next intersection, take the right fork and cross Rhine Creek. Immediately after crossing the bridge, the trail forks. You go left, now heading away from the road across a wooden walkway. Another fork is reached about 400 feet after the last; take the left fork. In another hundred feet, take the right fork. The trail joins the Old Oakland Road, now a wide dirt path, at the edge of the park. You follow the

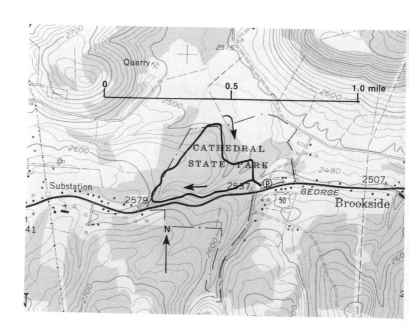

road for 200 feet and then follow Cathedral Trail to the right just before reaching Rhine Creek again. For a brief time you follow Partridge Berry Trail before it veers right. Go straight at this junction, and you will again be on Cathedral Trail. Another 300 feet and you encounter Giant Hemlock Trail coming in from the right.

Go straight here, crossing two bridges over Rhine Creek. After the second bridge, turn right and follow the trail back to the picnic ground and play area below the parking lot.

Tomlinson Run State Park: Laurel Trail

Distance: 1.7 miles
Time: 1 1/2 hours
Elevation change: 280 feet
Maps: USGS 7½′ East Liverpool South, Park map
Highlights: Mountain stream, view, spring wildflowers

Tomlinson Run State Park is at the northern tip of West Virginia's Northern Panhandle north of New Manchester on WV 8. The park includes 1,401 acres of steep hills and valleys centered on Tomlinson Run, a beautiful stream that has cut a deep gorge in its drop of approximately one hundred feet per mile to the Ohio River. In the past the entire area had been ravaged by coal mining and clear cutting of trees, as well as over-farmed and over-grazed. Today, this history is not obvious. During the depression years, the Works Progress Administration (WPA) set up a camp here where workers were given meals and crude shelter in exchange for manual labor. These workers constructed the park headquarters, superintendent's residence, picnic shelters, and roads, and foot trails. In addition, they made a dam on Tomlinson Run to control silt, creating a twenty-eight-acre lake.

The park is divided into two sections, the Activity Area and the Wilderness Area. The Activity Area includes facilities for camping, swimming, fishing, and boating as well as hiking. The Wilderness Area has been allowed to grow back so that now the hillsides and overhanging cliffs of sandstone and shale that flank

the gorge cut by Tomlinson Run are heavily forested. The second-growth trees are mostly oak, hickory, wild cherry, maple, beech, black birch, hemlock, and ash. The lush understory includes rhododendron, laurel, ferns, and numerous wildflowers. Laurel Trail, which features the gorge in the Wilderness Area, is reached by following the main park road 1.9 miles until it dead-ends at an intersection with unmarked WV 3 crossing Tomlinson Run. The trailhead is 200 yards to the right of the intersection, and the trail ends in the Boy Scout camp across the bridge just to the left of the intersection. Parking is available either across the road from the trailhead or at the bridge.

Laurel Trail is a loop marked by blue-blazed trees. The first half of the walk is relatively flat and therefore suitable for beginning hikers. The trail starts immediately up a short incline away from the road. It soon crests and follows the rim of the gorge cut by Tomlinson Run. As the grass-lined path traverses the gorge rim through a second-growth forest, you can look down on the birds flitting among the valley trees. In spring, you'll see carpets

Jack-in-the-pulpit

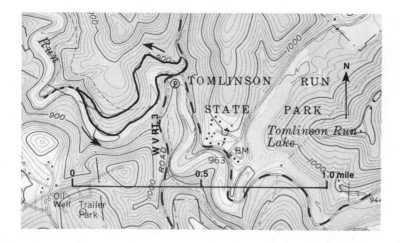

of trillium growing on the slopes across the narrow valley on the far side of Tomlinson Run.

The trail turns to the east and begins to descend one-half mile from the trailhead. An old road then intersects from the west. Follow the old road to the left as the return portion of a loop if you are an adventurous hiker, or retrace your steps for an easier route. If you cross a culvert, you have gone beyond Laurel Trail. Beyond the culvert, the trail is marked by white-blazed trees and is called the White Oak Trail. This trail was closed at the time of our latest visit (1984).

The return loop route involves scrambling over a landslide across the path, navigating a narrow and sometimes soggy route along the steep stream bank, and fording Tomlinson Run at the Boy Scout camp. The effort is rewarded by a closeup view of Tomlinson Run, a beautiful waterfall on a tributary, and a spectacular population of jack-in-the-pulpit.

You may know that by bending low or flipping up the "hood" of the flower you may observe "Jack" standing in his pulpit. You may not know, however, that Jack actually may be male or female. In fact, a particular plant may be male in one year and female the next. This curious ability to switch sexes has spawned no small measure of scientific interest in jack-in-the-pulpit because sexuality, and the ability to change sex, may have all sorts of evolutionary implications. Little is known about how such a breeding system evolved, or what triggers the sex-switching, but the sermons of this humble little understory plant will undoubtedly provide some answers.

Core Arboretum

Distance: 2 miles
Time: 30-45 minutes
Elevation change: 200 feet
Maps: USGS 7½' Morgantown North, Arboretum map
Highlights: Third largest Chinkapin Oak in world, identified
 plants, spring wildflowers

The Core Arboretum is a seventy-five acre tract of land located on the east bank of the Monongahela River in Morgantown. It is accessible from Monongahela Boulevard (US 19, WV 7) near the West Virginia University Evansdale Campus. Parking is available in the lot at the arboretum entrance.

The arboretum is owned and maintained by the Department of Biology at West Virginia University for use by researchers and the general public. The entrance is a beautifully maintained grassy glade with labeled native and non-native plants. A well-marked system of trails traverses a mixed hardwood forest that slopes steeply to the river flood plain. Many of the trees and shrubs along the trails are labeled, making the walk more fun for those interested in plant identification.

The arboretum is especially beautiful when the spring wildflowers are at their peak in April and May. Jeffersonia and bloodroot grow right up to the edge of the trail. Virginia bluebells form lush vibrant blue carpets near the base of the steep slope north of the railroad tracks. Trout lilies, trillium, and Dutchman's-breeches form large spring flower

gardens along portions of the trail's edge. Spring beauties and violets inhabit the grassy meadows along the trail.

Weekend spring wildflower hikes are led annually by members of the West Virginia University biology department. These tours traditionally are scheduled on the last three Sundays in April. Information on these events is available from the biology department.

The loop hike described here follows parts of the Strausbaugh, Sheldon, Granville Island, Rumsey, and Taylor Trails. The trails are well marked with wooden signs posted on trees. Upon entering the wooden archway of the arboretum, walk to the right toward a glass display case with a map showing the possible routes. Take the Strausbaugh Trail (the right fork). After about a hundred yards the trail starts downhill toward the river. In the spring this section of the path is lined with carpets of spring beauties, cut-leaved toothwort, twinleaf, hepatica, Virginia bluebells, Dutchman's-breeches, trout lily, trillium, bloodroot, and other ephemeral spring wildflowers.

Follow the Strausbaugh Trail until it reaches a dead end with a "trail closed" sign. Then take the Sheldon Trail turning downhill to the left. At the bottom of the slope, you reach the Granville Island Trail. At this junction stands a magnificent chinkapin oak. It is five feet-three inches in diameter, the largest individual of the species in West Virginia and the third largest in the world (in diameter). (The two larger trees are in Ohio.) The tops are broken off in all three. Perhaps when the tops do not break, the trees grow so top-heavy that they become vulnerable to high winds and blow down before they have a chance to reach the size of this large specimen.

Circle clockwise around the base of this tree, and you are on the Granville Island Trail. This trail parallels a railroad track flanked by carpets of Virginia bluebells. It then crosses the track and dips onto the river flood plain. There is a fork in the trail before a lagoon, where you can take either path. The right fork follows the riverbank, while the left fork (or the Nuttall Trail) runs along the lagoon.

The lagoon vibrates with spring life. Wood ducks have been known to nest in this lagoon, and in spring you may happen upon a duck family cruising along

White trillium

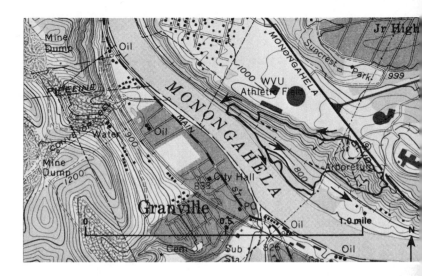

the edge, red-eared turtles basking on a drowned tree limb, or goldfish and brown carp mating in the shallows. The lagoon was once an arm of the river, when the land between the lagoon and the river was called Granville Island.

At the southwest end of the lagoon the Granville Island Trail turns away from the river to rejoin the Nuttall Trail. Before this point you will see an unofficial trail continuing along the river and crossing under a power line. Follow the main trail straight ahead across the railroad tracks.

After you cross the tracks, take the right fork, or the Rumsey Trail, and continue along above the tracks. The next junction is with a service road to the left and the Taylor Trail.

Take the Taylor Trail, which ascends the right slope of a steep drainage gulch while the Rumsey Trail ascends the left slope. The Taylor Trail forks twice more on the way back up the main slope. Take the right fork each time, and you will find your way back into the wooded glade and the parking lot.

Audra State Park: Alum Cave Trail

Distance: 2.3 miles
Time: 1 1/2 hours
Elevation change: 700 feet
Maps: USGS 7½′ Audra, Park map
Highlights: Views of cliffs, views of Middle Fork River

Audra is a small but beautiful state park on the banks of the Middle Fork River. Its lush forest includes massive rhododendron thickets, large oaks and hemlocks flanked with mosses, and wild-flowers. The 355-acre park is located between Philippi and Buckhannon. Signs along WV 119 indicate the way. Turn southeast off WV 119 on County Route 36. This road joins County Route 11, where a sign leads you to the park entrance six miles from WV 119. To reach Alum Cave Trail, turn left after entering the park, and cross the bridge over the Middle Fork River. Park your car in the first parking lot on the right. The trailhead is across the park road, behind the swimming area.

The beginning of the trail is paved and leads to a picnic area and playground. Soon it turns into a dirt path that weaves through huge stands of rhododendron along the riverbank. Rest benches and stone-pillared guardrails make this portion of the hike suitable for hikers of any ability. The trail leads to a large rock outcrop decorated with caps of moss and rhododendron. The trail then crosses a wooden bridge over a small drainage and intersects with a trail coming from upslope and leading toward the river.

Take the left fork, which follows the river, skirting underneath the cliff along a boardwalk.

This portion of the hike is very impressive. On one side of the path is a massive overhanging cliff, and on the other side is the river. In spring, the river is wild whitewater frothing around big boulders and over ledges. In summer, the water is crystal clear and inviting.

Just beyond this point, the hike has a difficult spot. The trail leads through large boulders forming a trench and climbs up a set of slippery rotten stairs with steps missing. Ignore the short spur trail toward the river at the bottom of the stairs, and ascend the stairs with care. At the top of the stairs, the trail intersects with another path. Take the route to the left along the river. Two switchbacks take you closer to the river through lush forests of rhododendron and large hardwoods. Many short spurs to the left offer views of the river. The main trail climbs moderately and joins another path coming in from the right, then dips down to skirt the river.

You may see patches of dead or dying rhododendron. The dieback is thought to

Middle Fork

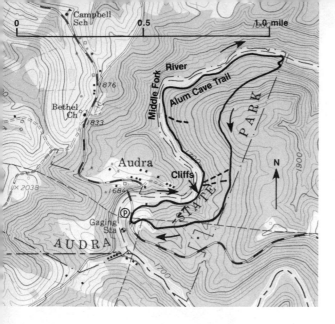

be due to a root fungus, because above the base of a single stem all branches are affected. Shoot or leaf diseases more often can affect some portions of the crown without affecting all of it. The rhododendron dieback is quite common in West Virginia, and entire stands may be devastated. The rhododendron, however, is not defenseless; it may grow back vigorously by sprouting from the base, thereby regaining its dominance in the understory.

The path continues along the river, bypassing a trail that veers to the right up worn wood-terraced stairs. Hikers can enjoy this portion of the trail in solitude, as it seems rarely used. The trail returns with a sharp right 1.3 miles from the trailhead. If the path dead-ends at the river, you've missed the turn. A tree ringed by two blue stripes is a marker noting that you've gone a couple of yards too far.

The return path threads through a marvelous forest of huge trees. The forest floor is carpeted with pink striped wood

sorrel, jewelweed, and scattered lady slippers. As the path leads up and away from the river, it weaves among large boulders along a couple of switchbacks. In spring and early summer, the song of the wood thrush penetrates the stillness above the sound of the river.

The path continues back up the river above the path leading downriver. A trail joins the path from the right coming up from below. You continue straight to a picnic area, passing some outhouses that may be seen through the trees on the left. Approximately two miles from the trailhead, the trail intersects a paved road in the picnic area. Turn right along the paved road for a short distance. Then take the wide path leading off to the right, between a water fountain and a rest bench, and through a horseshoe court. Follow it to the bottom of the hill, then turn right and you will be in a parking lot. At the far end of the lot is the main road. Turn right and return to your car in the lower lot.

Cedar Creek State Park

Distance: 3.2 miles
Time: 3 hours
Elevation change: 740 feet
Maps: USGS 7½' Tanner, Glenville; Park map
Highlight: Stone trough

Cedar Creek State Park lies in the foothills of the Allegheny Mountains in central West Virginia. The park encompasses 2,395 acres situated around Cedar Creek, which offers muskellunge and bass fishing as well as swimming.

To reach Cedar Creek State Park and the hiking trail we describe, take US 33 and 119 for three miles south of Glenville. Following Cedar Creek State Park signs, turn southeast from the highway and go four miles to the park entrance. From the park entrance, follow the signs to the campground, taking a right at the intersection. The trailhead is 2.4 miles from the park entrance. Do not be confused by a sign at Campsite T7 for a trailhead to Stone Trough Trail; this is the end of the "short" loop. The trail we describe begins opposite a bathhouse, where parking is available nearby.

The trailhead is at the far end of the clearing of Campsite T3. The trail is blazed with red paint. Almost immediately you encounter a fairly steep ascent along the right bank of a gulch. The trail next crosses what looks like an old railroad bed, then traverses the slope to the left. With a couple of switchbacks, the path leads upslope through a middle-aged forest.

This forest, like those in most of the park, is predominantly oak and tulip poplar. These forests serve as game refuges for deer, rabbits, squirrels, groundhogs, chipmunks, grouse, and quail. No hunting is permitted. The edges of the path harbor blueberry bushes that provide food for wild game as well as for hikers. Here the game animals far outnumber the hikers. Not another soul was seen along the entire route as we hiked the trail on Memorial Day, although the campground was filled to overflowing.

The path levels out and quickly bends right after 0.5 mile, following the contour of the ridge. Stargrass, bluets, and blue-eyed grass speckle the trail with dots of yellow and blue. Hikers must be careful to follow the red blazes, for numerous old and long-abandoned roads crisscross the trail. Where the path begins to climb again, wild comfrey grows in the trail. This plant sends up a spire of blue funnel-shaped flowers from a base of numerous large rough leaves. The spirally coiled inflorescence straightens out as the flowers open. Herbalists have used a close relative of this plant as an anesthetic, applying the crushed leaves to hemorrhoids. From the look of the rough leaves, modern remedies must be preferable by far! At the top of the ridge, the path winds

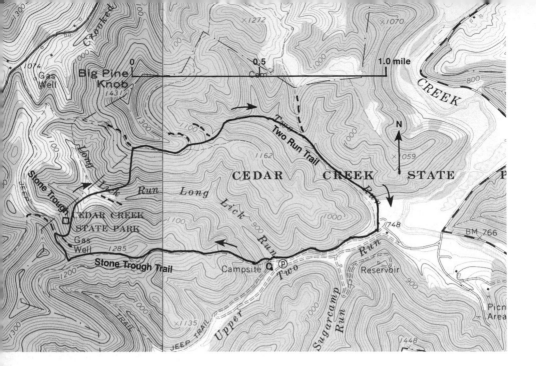

through a wind-stunted forest of chestnut oak mixed with Virginia pine. During the leafless season, you will enjoy a nice view. After following the ridgetop for a short distance, the path turns right and dips downhill. Note this point, for 200 yards beyond it you will need to follow a sharp right turn. If you miss the sharp right, the red blazes stop and the path becomes overgrown. The right turn appears to lead to a gas line. Here again, be alert to catch a small trail blazed in red, going off to the left downhill. This left turn occurs well before you get to the gas line clearing, but it is easy to miss.

The old stone trough for which the trail is named is found along this portion of the trail. It is a watering trough for livestock that was hand carved from solid rock, and it is believed to be well over a hundred years old. Although it is small and of simple design, the trough must have taken a great deal of time and hard labor to make with the tools available in the 1800s.

The trail descends from the old stone trough to follow a barbed wire fenceline bordering a meadow becoming overgrown. The diversity of habitats in this portion of the trail offer good bird watching. Blue-winged warblers may be heard and seen perched in the trees along the meadow's edge in spring. The buzzy notes of a cerulean warbler may rise above the sound of the brook in the bottom land. Soon after the path leaves the fence, it intersects with Two Run Trail. If you wish to shorten your hike, take the trail straight ahead back to the campground. We describe the longer route to the left along Two Run Trail.

Two Run Trail is blazed in white. It immediately fords a small stream, climbing fairly steeply as it leaves the stream. Take a right turn at an intersection with a wide jeep trail. Sandstone cliffs flank the upper side of the trail. An operating oil well with a large holding tank is encoun-

The Stone Trough

tered along this portion of the hike. The trail passes the well and continues parallel to the ridge crest through open beech and maple woods. The ridge crest descends to the level of the trail, and a small road goes off to the left around the ridge while Two Run Trail continues straight.

If you keep a sharp lookout on the forest floor, you may discover an Eastern box turtle wandering about in search of a mate or food. These reptiles are remarkable in several ways. Box turtles have been known to live for over a century, and it is probably not uncommon for them to reach sixty years of age. They feed on wild berries, insects, and earthworms. Being cold-blooded, box turtles have a slow metabolism and can readily survive a year's fast. They will eat frequently, however, when food is available, storing the surplus nourishment as fat as humans do.

Colors at the red end of the spectrum are easiest for turtles to sense, and these colors most frequently adorn the turtles themselves. The male Eastern box turtle usually has red eyes, while a female's eyes are brown. It seems female box turtles have a sexual preference for red-eyed males. Box turtles, unlike many wild animals, are very docile and make good pets. At first, they are shy, heads retreating into their shells at your approach, but after a while they make themselves at home. Many a child has gained a first-hand appreciation of nature by making friends with a box turtle. Fortunately for the turtle, captivity is usually short-lived, as afternoon walks in the grass eventual-ly present a chance to escape. In the end, box turtles, like all wild animals, would rather be free.

Two Run Trail takes an abrupt right turn around a large beech with a white blaze. This turn is easy to miss but if you do go too far, the trail peters out noticeably, and you can retrace your steps. This portion of the path leads down a bank to a stream, then along the stream to a confluence of two streams, which is what gives the trail and the stream below this point their name. The path follows this pretty stream through a forest of large buckeyes and beeches interspersed with grassy glades. Wild iris and stonecrop grow along the edge of the trail.

Just beyond a point where the path fords the stream is the intersection with North Boundary Trail. Continue to the right along Two Run Trail. (North Boundary Trail was not maintained in 1984.) Two Run Trail continues to follow Two Run to a point just before a pond. Here the trail takes a steep right turn and ascends a slope skirting the pond. Maidenhair ferns grace the path. The trail wanders out of the forest into the park superintendent's back yard beside a series of ponds. It then follows the edge of the woods before reaching the park road.

If you wish, you can follow the park road to the right, back to your car. Alternatively, take a right on the trail that is found between the stream and the woods. This trail parallels the road, leading back to the camping area where your vehicle is parked.

North Bend State Park

Distance: 3.6 miles
Time: 4 hours
Elevation change: 1,520 feet
Maps: USGS 7½' Harrisville, Park map
Highlights: Excellent birding, lush river-bottom forest

North Bend State Park is located twenty-eight miles east of Parkersburg in the northwestern part of West Virginia. It lies in the broad valley of the North Fork of the Hughes River. A northern horseshoe bend in the river gives the park its name. Hardwood forests cover the steep rocky ridges and the lush moist river-bottoms of the park's 1,405 acres. The history of an oil industry is written on the hills with relics such as rusted oil rigs and the silent remains of heavy equipment scattered beneath the trees.

Activities in the park include swimming, fishing, tennis, miniature golf, camping, and hiking. The campground is nestled in a grassy bend beside the tree-lined Hughes River. Its pastoral setting and fresh, well-groomed appearance make it one of the more popular camping areas in West Virginia. Despite the popularity of the campground, the trails are not heavily used. One exception is a paved hiking trail (not described here) called "The Extra Mile," which has been developed especially for the blind and wheelchair-bound.

If you are traveling from the east toward Parkersburg, you can reach North Bend State Park and the hike we describe by taking the Ellenboro exit off US 50 east of Parkersburg. Then follow WV 31 south to Harrisville, where you take WV 5 west to the park entrance three miles from Harrisville. Alternatively, if you are coming from the west, take the Cairo exit from US 50. Then follow WV 31 through Cairo, where one mile past Cairo you can take WV 5 east to the park. From the main park entrance, follow the signs for the campground and swimming area. Go to the pond at the camping area beyond the spur road to the pool, and park opposite the outhouses. This will be 0.2 mile past the swimming area spur road and 1.2 miles from the park entrance.

The trailhead is across the road from the outhouses. Use the footbridge to cross the small tributary. Where the path immediately forks, you take the right fork, following the riverbank. The trail wanders along the riverbank through a lush forest of large, widely spaced beeches, buckeyes, and hemlocks. In the early spring, the spires of thick creamy buckeye blossoms are frequented by ruby-throated hummingbirds.

You'll have a chance to see a variety of birds as the trail travels through the different habitats of riverbank and upland dry forest, but the ruby-throated hum-

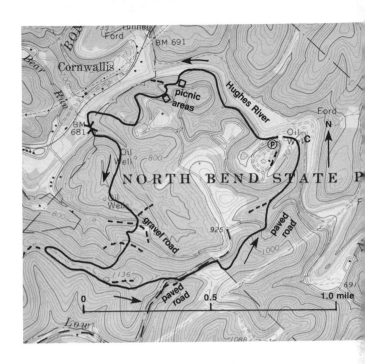

mingbird is one of the most fascinating. It is our smallest bird, only three and a half inches long. The bill accounts for about one and a half inches of the total length. Because it is so small and because its feeding habits are similar to some insects, especially the hawk moth, they are sometimes confused. Flower nectar extracted by the long bill is the main food of the hummingbird, supplemented with insects and small spiders. Not a calorie-watcher, the average hummingbird consumes half its weight in sugar daily!

There are several species of hummingbirds in North America, but the ruby-throated hummingbird is the only one found in the east. Believe it or not, the hummingbird is closely related to the woodpecker. Its unique wings have a "reverse" gear that allows it to fly backward, and it is the only bird that can hover without body motion. The ruby-throated hummingbird had few natural

Morel mushroom

enemies until the introduction from Europe of the insect-eating praying mantis. Perhaps praying mantises confuse the tiny birds with the hawk moth too. Praying mantises have been seen to grasp hapless hummingbirds by their necks and kill them as they fed among the garden flowers. Most other animals, though, beat a hasty retreat when confronted by the feisty little birds. A prod or two from the sharp beak is enough to displace even large bumblebees from a flower that a ruby-throated hummingbird covets.

At a "TRAIL" sign that points away from the river, the trail veers up the slope away from the river and comes up behind a picnic area. Go right, behind the picnic shelter and into a pine and hemlock stand to pick up the trail again. The trail soon intersects with a trail coming in from the right. Take a sharp left, and follow the contour of the ravine around to the right, coming up behind a second picnic shelter. The right fork of the intersecting trail would lead you back down to the riverbank. If you are a connoisseur of morel mushrooms, and the season is right, you may find them here.

Walk through this picnic area toward the rest rooms, and take the trail just to the right of the rest rooms, which continues in the same direction you have been going. The path descends to the river where you can see a railroad track and a house on the opposite bank. This portion of the path is not frequently used. The trail then goes under a power line and comes to a small tributary crossed by a wooden bridge. The trail then follows the left bank of the stream up a hill, continuing to the ridge crest through a young mixed hardwood forest.

The ridge top is upland forest of mixed hardwood and second-growth pine. Follow the trail south to the end of the ridge, where you will cross an old vehicle track, then descend to a gravel road. Here you follow the road to the left for seventy to eighty feet to find the trail leaving the other side of the road beside an unmarked wooden post. Occasional red blazes mark the trail. About a hundred yards into the woods, the trail turns to the right and parallels the road. You will see a nice rock outcrop on the left with an overhang that affords shelter from the weather. The path circles around the outcrop and ascends to the top of the ridge.

A trail crosses the path about 0.3 mile after the intersection with the gravel road. Ignore it, and continue straight ahead.

As you reach the top of the ridge, the path bends back toward the east and follows the ridge. Within a hundred yards after gaining the ridge crest, the path joins an old vehicle track. Continue along in the same direction. Next an old road leaving to the left toward the knob of the hill also should be ignored. The trail leads to a paved road immediately after it passes an abandoned oil well. Turn left on the old vehicle track (northeast) and parallel the paved road. Within forty yards you turn right onto a foottrail.

This trail follows the road, emerging in an overgrown field. Walk through the field, staying close to the guardrail. At a break in the guardrail, the trail turns right, crosses the road and climbs up steps on the opposite side. The path then traverses the slope above the road, before dipping down to cross another paved road. From here the path descends from the paved road beside a curve sign, turning left after about one hundred yards to cross a small stream. After ascending the slope on the opposite side, the path joins a well-worn trail coming in from the west and continues to the right along the ridge top. After about 0.4 mile you finally descend into the campground near the pond.

7

Holly River State Park: Potato Knob Trail

Distance: 3.7 miles
Time: 3 hours
Elevation change: 760 feet
Maps: USGS 7½′ Goshen; Park map
Highlights: Views, waterfalls, cliffs

Potato Knob Trail is at the southern tip of Holly River State Park. The main entrance to the park is thirty-four miles south of Buckhannon on WV 20. To reach Potato Knob Trail, turn east off WV 20 1.3 miles south of the main park entrance, onto Left Fork Holley River Road. At 0.1 mile the road crosses a bridge over Laurel Fork, and at 0.2 mile the paved road becomes a well-graded gravel road. After following this road for four miles from WV 20, watch for a small road going off to the right marked by a sign that says "Falls." Follow this side road about 200 yards to an abrupt fork in the road. Park your car near the fork in the road. The left fork, which leads to Potato Knob Trail, is recommended for foot traffic only.

Signs point to the "Upper Falls" (a small trail to the left off the steep graveled road) and to the "Chute." Follow signs to the Chute to reach Potato Knob Trail. The Upper Falls, only a short 200-yard side jaunt down a well-marked path, is well worth the trip on the way. The falls are about fifteen feet high, with a natural pool carved below them by the force of the cascading water.

The road to the Chute and to Potato Knob descends through a deciduous hardwood forest of oaks, tulip poplars,

and occasional umbrella magnolias, with an understory of rhododendron. Continue walking downhill until you reach a small parking area at 0.3 mile. You reach a trail junction here with signs pointing straight ahead to Potato Knob Trail and also to the right up a steep slope.

The trail to the right, which ascends Potato Knob and is marked with red blazes, should be attempted only by hikers who are in good condition. It climbs very steeply up a forested ridge, reaching a twenty-foot rock outcrop at 0.5 mile. Curiously, here on the steep and typically dry slope, you encounter a stand of hemlock and rhododendron, plants more typical of streamsides. At 0.7 mile the trail bends to the right under another rock face. On the far side of the face the trail turns sharply left and upward near a rhododendron thicket. At the next rock ledge the trail goes left, eventually traversing under a large overhanging ledge. Reaching the end of the ledge, the trail circles right, climbing steeply to the top of the ledge that you just walked under. Nice views greet you at an overlook on the right side of the trail.

Here the trail splits, with red blazes leading straight ahead and another unmarked trail heading to the right. The red-blazed trail leads toward the true

Northern Hills Province

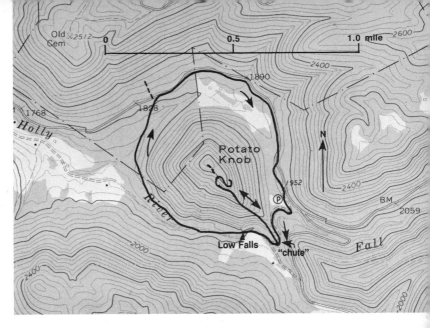

summit of Potato Knob, but the blazes and the trail become obscure within 0.2 mile of the junction. The best views can be reached by following the unmarked trail to the right at the junction. This trail leads to a superb overlook at 0.9 mile with a 270-degree view of the surrounding countryside.

The overlook is a great place to catch your breath, rest, and munch on a snack. You may hear the high-pitched whistle of a hawk as it soars at eye level between the peaks. If the wind is just right, you may also catch the sound of the rushing river in the valley bottom. After experiencing the exhilarating climb and the fine view, you may think the name Potato Knob, even though it is descriptive, seems far too modest.

To continue the hike, retrace your steps (carefully) down to the first trail junction at 1.5 miles. To limit your outing to the Knob climb, of course you can turn left at the junction up the gravel road to your car (round-trip distance, 1.8 miles). Alternatively, for a loop hike, fol-

Looking down on the trees from the overlook

low the Potato Knob Trail to the right. Be sure to take the short spur trail toward the stream to see the Chute as well. The Chute is an unusual narrow and winding trench where Fall Run has carved through bedrock to join the Left Fork of Holly River. Potato Knob Trail quickly joins Holly River also, turning right and following the river downstream toward "Low Falls."

At 1.7 miles the trail reaches Low Falls, where Holly River plunges over an eight-foot ledge into a pool. Below Low Falls the stream drops over a series of ledges while the trail follows on the steep bank. At 2.2 miles you encounter a No Trespassing sign indicating that the land to your left is private. The trail crosses to the right of a small clearing, and at 2.4 miles it veers away from the river. Here the trail follows an old railroad grade. The trail crosses a small stream at 2.5 miles and then becomes very rocky through an open woods.

At 2.7 miles the trail ascends to the Left Fork Holly River Road (sign spells it "Holley"). Here you turn right and follow the road one mile back to the turnoff marked by the "Falls" sign.

Kumbrabow State Forest

Distance: 4.2 miles
Time: 3 to 3 1/2 hours
Elevation change: 880 feet
Maps: USGS 7½′ Adolph, Forest map
Highlights: Wildflowers, old forest, view

Kumbrabow is one of the most remote tracts of state land in West Virginia and perhaps one of the least visited. From the hiker's point of view, however, the trip is worthwhile. The entire state forest (9,431 acres) lies above 2,500 feet in elevation, so spring comes late, fall comes early, and in summer Kumbrabow offers a cool escape from hot weather. The name of the forest is derived from the names of three families—Kump, Brady, and Bowers—who originally owned much of the land and worked to insure its preservation as a state forest.

The state forest is reached by a gravel access road that turns off WV 219 eight miles south of Huttonsville. Follow the gravel road 3.5 miles to the state forest entrance, then drive another 3.1 miles to a small picnic ground on the left side of the road where you can park. You'll find the trailhead across the road from the picnic ground. The trail parallels the south bank of the stream named Meatbox Run. "Run" is synonymous with "stream" in this part of the country. The path gradually ascends above the valley bottom through a beautiful forest of mixed hardwoods and occasional evergreens.

Large birches, maples, beeches, hem-

locks, and red spruces attest to the undisturbed nature of the woods. Mixed in with these giants are their offspring, so the forest contains not only a rich variety of dominant species, but also a mixture of ages of trees. While this may not strike you as unusual, in fact it is becoming uncommon in eastern forests because of an extensive history of disturbance—primarily logging. In disturbed forests, most of the trees will be nearly the same age, because they were established in the short favorable period after the disturbance. Another contrast is that in undisturbed forests the forest floor is often rich in species. In late May and early June here you will find jack-in-the-pulpits, Dutchman's-breeches, Indian cucumber, and orchids scattered in the understory. As you ascend farther, veritable carpets of ramps and trout lilies flank the trail.

The ascent becomes steep as you approach the top of a ridge. Meatbox Trail joins an old jeep trail near the top of the ridge (at 1.4 to 1.5 miles). Follow the jeep trail west about 360 yards until it intersects with Rich Mountain Fire Trail. Turn northeast, following the fire trail along the ridge. The fire trail was proba-

Vibernum

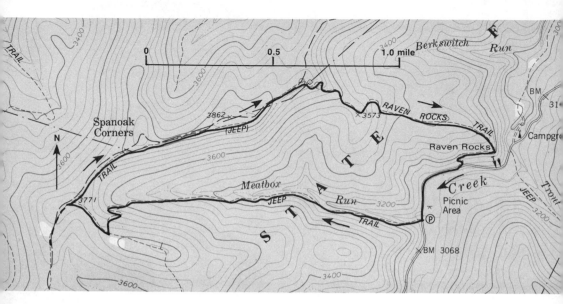

bly built to provide access for firecrews controlling forest fires in the area. Raven Rocks Trail leaves the fire trail to the right at a cement signpost 1.3 miles beyond the intersection of Meatbox Trail.

Follow Raven Rocks Trail back down the ridge toward the state forest road. Before reaching the road the trail leads through a tunnel of rhododendrons to Raven Rocks Overlook. The overlook provides a good view of the valley cut by Mill Creek, of which Meatbox Run is a tributary. To the north is the entrance to the state forest and to the south is the state forest road leading to Pickens. From the overlook, the trail descends steeply to the road. Turn right and follow the road 0.3 mile to return to the picnic area and your car.

Coopers Rock State Forest

Distance: 4.5 miles
Time: 3 hours
Elevation change: 600 feet
Maps: USGS 7½' Lake Lynn
Highlight: Henry Clay Furnace

Coopers Rock State Forest is a well-known scenic attraction perched high above the valley formed by the Cheat River. The Coopers Rock Scenic Overlook attracts thousands of visitors annually, and it is worth a stop if you are in the area. Access to the state forest is via Exit 13 off US 48, ten miles east of Morgantown. The main road into the state forest heads south from the exit, winding for 3.1 miles along the top of Chestnut Ridge where it reaches a dead end at the overlook. Within a short walk from the overlook parking lot, you can gaze down on the emerald-green Cheat River as it winds its way through a veritable canyon 1,200 feet below the lookout before entering Cheat Lake. The view to the west is superb, giving a feeling of an endless jumble of rolling hills, all of about the same elevation.

The Henry Clay Furnace Trail that we describe begins near the entrance to the state forest 0.3 mile from the US 48 exit. It was built originally as a cross-country ski trail by the YACC in 1978, and with good snow conditions it is still used as such in the winter months. It is used for hiking in summer less frequently than other more popular short trails in the state forest and therefore provides for a nice, quiet morning or afternoon walk.

Our route to the Henry Clay Furnace begins near the wooden sign showing a rough map of the ski trails. Park your car in the lot located near the start of the ski trails. Follow the "easy" trail (shown in green on the sign) for 0.5 mile through a stand of mixed hardwoods (oak, cherry, and tulip tree). The trail then emerges into a grassy clearing and you pass a gravel road. Go down the steep embankment on the far side of the road behind a blue ski trail sign. After you hike into the woods 150 yards, the trail forks left or goes straight ahead. We will describe the route down to the furnace via the left fork. On skis, this clockwise route may be preferable because of the steady even climb of the return path in comparison with the irregular terrain on the way down to the furnace.

The trail is clearly marked with blue skiers painted on the trees along the way. Shortly after taking the left fork you pass under a small power line. You cross a bridge over a small stream after another short downhill stretch, and just beyond the stream you will find another trail junction. Follow the black trail signs straight ahead to the Henry Clay Furnace. After ascending a small ridge, you will walk

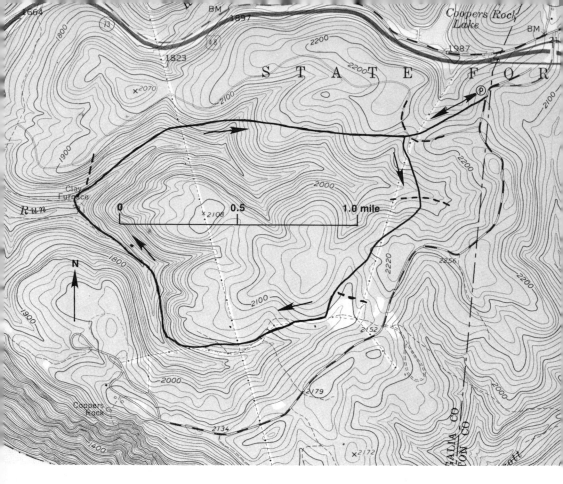

under the power line again. About 0.3 mile beyond the power line, a small trail joins the main trail from the left. Stay on the main trail.

Soon you begin a traverse down a gentle slope, and a manmade pond may be seen through the woods to the left of your path. At the bottom of the hill, the ski trail to the furnace parallels and sometimes follows a second power line for about 0.5 mile. When the trail leaves the power line, you begin a descent along the side of a valley through a nice stand of hemlock and rhododendron. A few large beech trees are scattered on the hillside as well.

Occasionally, you may notice large gray and rust-brown colored stumps on either side of the trail, standing like ghosts among the living trees. These are the remains of a formerly widespread dominant tree of the eastern deciduous forest: the American chestnut. This dethroned monarch met its nemesis earlier this century with the importation of a fungal blight from Europe. Some stumps still produce new sprouts, but the vast majority of chestnut saplings die before reproducing by seed so the species remains on the brink of extinction. One can only imagine how this magnificent tree might have made a very different experience for those hiking down this hollow seventy-five years ago.

The path at last descends to the valley bottom, where you will follow the stream

Henry Clay Furnace

(the south fork of Clay Run) for 0.3 miles to the Henry Clay Furnace. The furnace is reached by crossing a footbridge into a clearing. An interpretive sign beside the large stone furnace gives the history of the site, which dates to 1834. The furnace produced pig iron from local ore deposits for a period of eleven years. During its short useful life, a town of 200 people with more than 100 dwellings, reportedly called "Cooperstown," thrived at the site. Now, Cooperstown is a true ghost town, with only the furnace and a few scattered foundation stones to remind us of its history.

The return trail is found by following a service road up a hill to the right behind the furnace. There, the blue marker of a cross-country ski trail may be found on the right side of the road. Turning right off the service road, the trail ascends the side of a valley at a steady, but moderate pitch in nearly a straight line. In 1.7 miles, you will find the trail junction where you turned left earlier. Straight ahead lies the gravel road. To return to your car, just retrace your steps on the "easy" trail.

If your principal interest is in visiting the furnace, you can drive to a closer point and then make a short hike down the service road. Back at the main state forest road, turn right onto a gravel road just beyond the ski trail map. The turnoff is well marked with a sign pointing to the Henry Clay Furnace. About three miles from the turnoff, the road reaches a deadend in a parking lot. From there the hike to the furnace is approximately 0.5 mile on the service road.

10

Holly River State Park: Tecumseh Falls

Distance: 9.2 miles
Time: 7 hours
Elevation change: 1,900 feet
Maps: USGS 7½' Hacker Valley, Goshen; Park map
Highlights: Tecumseh Falls, rock outcrops, mountain streams

For hikers, Holly River State Park is a jewel. It is one of the most beautiful spots for outdoor enjoyment in West Virginia. Excellent scenery, trout fishing, picnicking, camping, and hiking abound in the park. The park has primitive walk-in campsites as well as modern campsites and cabins. A variety of trails wind through the ridgetops and lowlands, and each trail has special highlights. The trails are well-kept yet lightly traveled. Quite probably you may hike all day and encounter no one.

In addition to being one of the most beautiful areas of West Virginia, this is also one of the wettest. Holly River State Park is located thirty-four miles south of Buckhannon on WV 20 between Hacker Valley and Pickens. The town of Pickens, just ten miles east of the park, is notorious as West Virginia's rainiest spot. Average annual precipitation is sixty-six inches. Pickens also holds the record in West Virginia for the highest average snowfall per year. Summer and fall are the driest seasons for fair-weather hikers. In spring, the streams are racing, the waterfalls are full and powerful, and the wildflowers and birds are at their peak.

The beginning of the day hike we describe is reached by following the park road from WV 20 to the entrance of the campground. Park there, and hike down the narrow, paved road through the camping area to campground #4. The road leads along the Laurel Fork, which is exceptionally pretty. The clear water tumbles over rock ledges into waist-deep pools. Large stands of rhododendron flank the stream, their gnarled branches arching down to the cool water.

As you hike down the road, always take the left-most fork, until the paved road ends in a loop at a ball field. A gravel road and a trail lead off the paved road on the left side of the loop away from the stream. Follow the white-blazed trail up the slope.

At first the trail ascends a moderate slope through small hardwoods, then it reaches the crest of the lower part of a ridge and bends left, following the crest of the ridge. This portion of the trail involves a steep climb through mature dry woods consisting of oaks, beeches, maples, and old ghosts of American chestnuts. The forest is probably about a century old in places. The path crests a hump in the flank, then traverses to the right of a rock outcrop spotted with

A snake fence

rhododendron and large oaks. The trail climbs on top of this backbone, then continues up higher and higher, and it is steep in sections.

Just when you think you've reached the top of the ridge, another steep section looms up in front of you. The trail finally crests a large knob, but there is no overlook here. The path descends steeply into a windblown saddle. Here dead grapevines are balled up like tumbleweed and caught behind trees. The forest floor is swept bare of leaves except behind dead snags and boulders that have created wind blocks.

Upon climbing to the top of a second large knob, you are rewarded with a nice view of the valley created by Laurel Fork. The trail continues along the ridge crest. Remnants of an old snake fence wind among the trees. The trail ascends to the top of another knob that, like the first, has no view except occasional glimpses through the trees. The path then leads to a patrol cabin in a large meadow. You can camp here overnight if you make arrangements at the park headquarters.

The log cabin is quaint. A woodstove, a stash of firewood, a table and benches, and a sleeping loft make this an inviting place to rest or stay in bad weather. Deer are frequent visitors to the meadow. The trail, still marked by white-blazed trees, leaves the left side of the meadow. A stand of seedling red spruce may be seen on the right of the trail as it skirts to the left of a high knob. Morel mushrooms can be gathered here in season (April or May).

Next you encounter the intersection with Tremontane Trail, which is blazed in red and comes in from the left out of the valley. You continue to the right along the ridgetop, following red blazes. A road intersects from the right, then leaves the Tremontane Trail to the right. You continue to follow the red blazes leading along the left side of the ridgetop. Sever-

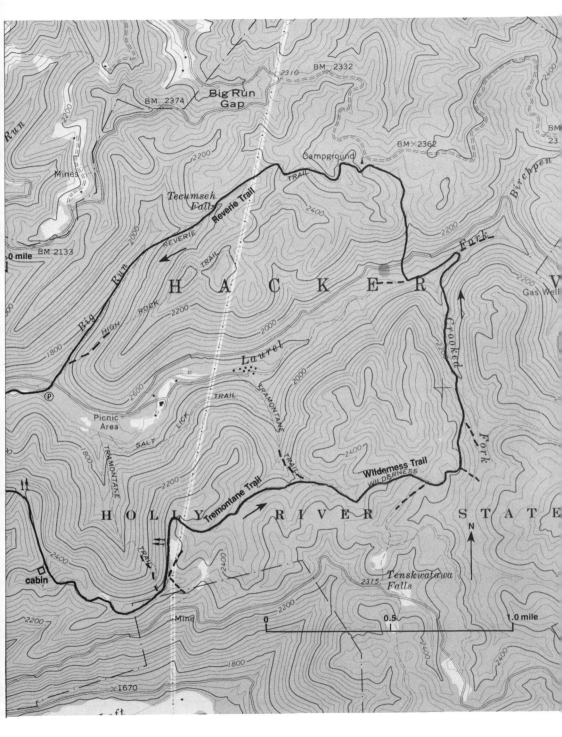

al small clearings are on the right of the trail. Just beyond the clearings, an overlook to the left gives a view of distant ridges. Next a logging road intersects; take the right fork following the red blazes down the mountain under a power line. The remains of a foundation and an enormous sugar maple tree mark the site of a farm dwelling that once nestled in the swale.

Beyond the confluence of several small streams below the old farm site, you reach the Wilderness Trail intersection. Turn right and follow the blue blazes. The trail gently ascends among scattered house-sized boulders. On the tops of the boulders are little islands of vegetation complete with trees. At the drainage head, off the trail to the left is an eighteen-foot cliff. This is a potential waterfall during a spring rain.

Potato Knob Trail intersection is reached 0.6 mile from the intersection with Wilderness Trail. Follow Wilderness Trail as it continues to the left, with the spur to Tenskwatawa Falls and Potato Knob Trail leading to the right. The next intersection is an overlook spur leading straight ahead, while your trail bears left. Care must be taken here to follow the blue-blazed trail to avoid an unplanned bushwhacking adventure. The "overlook" is not well-defined, and it is easy to overlook it and wander astray.

Wilderness Trail descends through moist woods where water pools beneath the trees in the rainy season. The boulders and tree bases are covered with thick moss. The spur to the fire tower and the Railroad Grade Trail intersects from the right. Take the left fork continuing along Wilderness Trail, which takes you beneath a large rock overhang drip-ping with water, ferns, and rhododendron. Jack-in-the-pulpits grow right on the edge of the rock outcrop. At the outcrop, the trail makes a sharp right and drops down to the stream. The stream drops quickly over rock ledges and large boulders creating small waterfalls. After crossing two wooden bridges, the trail intersects with Reverie Trail. Take the Reverie Trail (marked by yellow blazes). About 150 yards past the intersection, Reverie Trail crosses a gravel road and ascends to a primitive campsite within 0.5 mile through a mixed hardwood forest. The primitive campsite has a fireplace, picnic table, outhouse, and a fresh-water spring.

Reverie Trail goes through the campsite, past the spring, and up a steep hill. The path traverses the ridge, then descends to the highlight of Reverie Trail, Tecumseh Falls. Here, the trail leads behind the falls, and you can stand in a cave looking at the falling water from behind without getting wet. Reverie Trail descends from the falls to Dreamer's Meadow, which is a fern-filled clearing to the right of the trail.

Old logging roads may be noticed along the descent, but these should not cause any confusion, for the trail is well-marked with yellow blazes. The path may be soggy along much of the way below Dreamer's Meadow. A stream crosses the path 0.5 mile below the meadow, and sometimes the stream prefers the path to the original streambed. High Rock Trail intersects from the left near the end of Reverie Trail. Reverie Trail continues straight ahead and descends to the main park road. Across the road is the campground and your vehicle.

Southern Hills Province

11

Beech Fork State Park

Distance: 2.2 miles
Time: 2 hours
Elevation change: 680 feet
Maps: USGS 7½′ Winslow, Park map
Highlight: Excellent birdwatching

Beech Fork State Park is new and un-finished. It will be a resort-style park when complete. A major lodge, cabins, golf course, swimming pools, playgrounds, campgrounds and many other recreational facilities are in various stages of completion.

What sets Beech Fork State Park apart from most other West Virginia state parks is the huge campground, which is located on the perimeter of 760-acre Beech Fork Lake and has 275 campsites with modern conveniences. The hiker will appreciate the state park for its diversity of habitat, which in turn attracts a large variety of birds. During the spring warbler migration, the hike we describe is tops for birders.

Beech Fork State Park is south of Huntington. The easiest access is via WV 10 south from exit 11 of Interstate 64. Follow the park signs from WV 10. One possible route is from Mays Chapel, where you take Heath Creek Road east 3.3 miles to Winslow. From Winslow, take Long Branch Road northeast approximately 2.5 to 3 miles to the park. The trail we describe is called Lost Trail. It begins in Moxley Branch Camping Area, which is

Listening for the elusive warbler

the second left turn beyond the park office and concession stand. The spur road to the campground crosses a narrow portion of the lake, then enters the campsite area. Lost Trail is reached by taking the first right, then a left at the next fork by the bathhouse and a left at the third fork. Parking usually is available in an unoccupied site.

Lost Trail leaves the camping area across the creek south of the bathhouse, where a wooden bridge leads across the creek. The trail crosses a second wooden bridge and enters an early successional forest of young Virginia pine and tulip poplar entangled with grape-vine. The trail is well marked with blue blazes. Immediately after the second bridge, the trail bears right at a fork. This fork is the intersection of the return portion of the loop. Lost Trail skirts the lake edge for about 0.9 mile. Within 0.3 mile of the last intersection, a trail comes in from the left. Your loop route bears right to cross a third bridge.

In spring, bay-breasted warblers, blue-winged warblers, Blackburnian warblers, and many others are known to inhabit the area along the lake's edge. No other family of North American birds is so numerous and so challenging to birders

Beech Fork State Park **53**

as that of the American wood warblers. Warblers often travel in small flocks of several species. While the birder is struggling to identify one or two of the birds in a feeding party, four or five others are flickering against the light, skipping behind the leaves, and teasing the birder's eyes off into the shadows away from his focus. Warblers seem to fly in a ceaseless frenzy among the leaves and branches. Jack Connor, author of the article "Warbler Chasing" in Blair and Ketchum's *Country Journal*, aptly describes warbler watching as the "warbler four-count." That is "one, it lands on a branch; two, it snatches up an insect; three, it glances around; four, it flies. Stop, snatch, look, go.... From the birder's point of view, that usually translates as, 'Hey! What? Un.... Damn!' "

In the spring, this hike also has a wonderful variety of wildflowers. Among them are larkspur, sedum, twin-leaf, trillium, bloodroot, sweet William, and May apple. May apples grow so thickly they carpet the forest floor in places. The umbrellalike leaves catch the eye while the nodding cream-colored flowers hide beneath. The flowers develop into lemonlike berries that are edible when made into jams and jellies. May apples are known for their medicinal qualities, although the leaves and roots are poisonous if eaten

in quantity. Indians used the plant as a laxative. Colonists used it as a laxative and in the treatment of syphilis. A compound in the root has even been used in treating some types of tumors.

When Lost Trail reaches a point opposite the boat dock across the lake, it makes a sharp left bend and ascends the ridge. The trail is steep in places. Once the ridge crest is reached, the trail meanders along the top, offering glimpses of the lake through the trees. At a bend in the ridge, the trail dips down to the left, heads back toward the lake and joins a logging road. The path continues to bear left, leaving the logging road (do not follow the logging road to the right), and crosses a small creek in a clearing.

The next intersection at 1.7 miles is that with the lower section of the loop. Here, Lost Trail bears right and parallels a stream for a short distance, then turns left away from the stream and skirts the left side of the ridge. Ignore the small path intersecting from the right. The trail circles around the contour of the flank of the ridge sixty vertical feet below the summit, then plunges downhill, turning to the left, where you meet the first part of the loop at the second bridge. Here, you retrace your steps along Lost Trail to the campground and your vehicle.

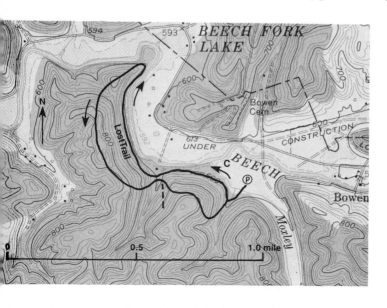

12

Babcock State Park

Distance: 2.3 miles
Time: 2 1/2 hours
Elevation change: 680 feet
Maps: USGS 7½' Danese; Park map
Highlights: Views, spring wildflowers

The focus of Babcock State Park is Glade Creek Grist Mill, which is in a picturesque setting on a large trout stream above a waterfall. The mill was pieced together with salvaged parts of old mills from across West Virginia. Freshly ground corn and buckwheat flour can be purchased at the mill. If you are there at the right time, you can watch your flour being made the old-fashioned way.

The park is very special for hiking during late May to early June. At this time of year, Catawba rhododendron, the lilac-purple rhododendron, is at its prime, and the trail system we describe is spectacular.

To reach Babcock State Park, take US 60 east from US 19 north of Beckley. After approximately seven miles, take WV 41 south for seven miles. The park has two entrances. The first is for a camping area. The second is the main entrance to the mill and the park office. To reach the trailhead, use the second entrance leading to the park office, and take the spur road to cabins one through six. Park across the road from cabin five at the beginning of Skyline Trail.

The Skyline Trail begins with stone steps up the hillside along a small stream. Hemlocks and mixed hardwood species form the forest canopy. Catawba rhododendron and numerous wildflowers make an impressive scene in the understory. The trail forks within a few hundred feet. Take the left fork, marked with a red blaze in the middle of a stone step. The right fork meanders up the stream, while Skyline Trail emerges out of a rhododendron thicket onto a cliff edge. From this point you can hear the roar of Glade Creek in the valley below. Beyond a wooden bridge is an overlook into Glade Creek Valley that is framed by purple blossoms in early June.

The trail returns to the rhododendron-lined forest and offers numerous views into the creek valley as it courses in and out of the forest along the cliff edge. A pair of switchbacks leads up to a clearing with a magnificent view of the New River Valley. Skyline Trail leaves the opposite side of the clearing, slightly downhill from where it entered. More spurs to the left of the trail offer glimpses into the gorge.

At the intersection with Rocky Trail 1.3 miles from the start, turn left. The red-blazed path going straight takes you to Mann's Creek picnic area. For a more leisurely or shorter hike, you can retrace your steps to your car at this point. As

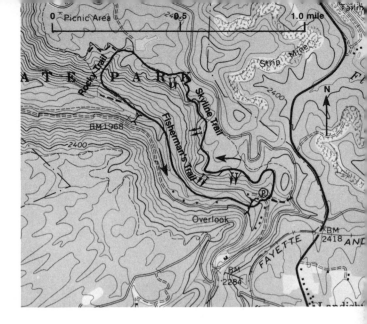

you go on, Rocky Trail is blazed with blue; it is aptly named, as it steps down the right bank of a small stream on rock ledges. The going is rough in parts, with a deteriorated bridge and fallen trees across the path.

At the bottom of the valley, the trail intersects with an old railroad bed. The old ties are still visible. At the valley bottom, turn left and hike up Glade Creek to a large bridge. Rocky Trail continues across the creek on the bridge. Here instead, take Fisherman's Trail, which follows along the creek without crossing the bridge. Fisherman's Trail is blazed in green.

If you like to fish, and you have your gear with you, undoubtedly you will want to try your luck in some of the deep holes. Glade Creek looks like one of those idyllic trout streams frequently shown in fishing magazines, but rarely seen in real life. Fisherman's Trail is rough going in places, involving scrambling over logs and boulders with little room between the creek and the mountainside. You find yourself practically in Glade Creek, as it roars over rock ledges and between huge water-worn boulders. The hike is beautiful, though, and well worth the scramble.

At the end, the trail comes out underneath another large bridge crossing the creek. Turn left on the bridge, and follow the stone walkway up to cabin five and your vehicle.

View of Glade Creek framed by
Catawba rhododendron

13

Grandview State Park

Distance: 2.3 miles
Time: 2 hours
Elevation change: 40 feet
Maps: USGS 7½' Prince; Park map
Highlight: Grand views

Perched above a sharp bend in the New River, Grandview is one of West Virginia's most scenic state parks. It is most famous for its outdoor amphitheater and nightly performances of the outdoor dramas, "Honey in the Rock" and "Hatfields and McCoys." "Honey in the Rock" tells a story of the birth of West Virginia during the Civil War, while "Hatfields and McCoys" portrays the feud between these two well-known mountain families.

To reach the park, follow US 19 to Beaver, five miles south of Beckley. Turn left off US 19 onto WV 9. The park is located at the terminus of WV 9, eleven miles north of Beaver. To reach the Canyon Rim trailhead, follow signs to the "main overlook." Park at the first lot you see, 0.1 mile from the park entrance.

Follow the stone path on the upper left side of the parking lot toward the main overlook. The numbered posts marking certain trees and shrubs along the way are part of a selfguided nature trail for which explanatory brochures are available at the park office. If you are a budding botanist, you may enjoy trying to identify the numbered plants before you check your identification in the park brochure. The area near the overlook is known for its spectacular rhododendrons,

which bloom profusely in May and June.

The promontory of the main overlook provides a breathtaking view of the canyon gouged out by the New River. New River, ironically, is one of the oldest rivers in North America. Formerly it was part of a massive river system that flowed north across the continent. It is the only remaining river that has its origin east of the Alleghenies (in the Blue Ridge) and cuts westward through the mountains, so the river you see below you at the overlook runs from right to left, from North Carolina northwest through West Virginia. The New joins the Gauley to form the Kanawha, which in turn flows into the Ohio, on to the Mississippi, and on to the Gulf of Mexico—a circuitous route indeed for a drop of water falling in the Blue Ridge Mountains!

Canyon Rim Trail provides level and easy walking suitable for hikers of any ability. From the main overlook, retrace your steps along the stone path and turn right (near post #12 on the selfguided trail), following the edge of the open area to the woodland trail that skirts the canyon rim. Trails coming in from the left are from a picnic area, while those to the

View of New River from Turkey Spur Rocks

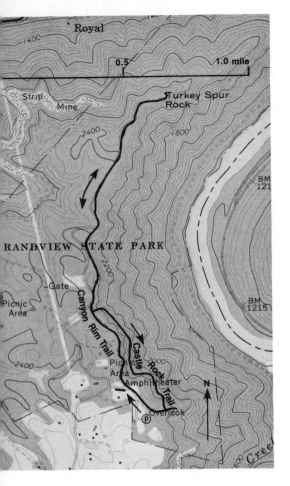

the trailhead.

Another 0.5 mile of walking along the road will bring you to Turkey Spur Rock. There, a small trail leads to the top of the rocks to another overlook. The path picks its way up through large crevices in the rock pinnacle that forms Turkey Spur. On the way up, you will pass "Nature's Air Conditioner"—a fissure in the cliff where cool air constantly flows down the rock face. On a hot day, you'll want to stand here and enjoy the refreshing breeze.

The overlook itself affords a spectacular view of the New River. From one vantage point, the New River seems to be two rivers flowing in opposite directions. This illusion is due to the sharp hairpin turn west of the overlook where the river doubles back on itself for over a distance of four miles with only half a mile of land between the two courses.

From here, retrace your steps along Canyon Rim Trail. For a more adventurous return trip, go left at the junction with Castle Rock Trail. Castle Rock Trail parallels Canyon Rim Trail, winding beneath expansive rock strata revealing an exposed coal seam, much like those being mined throughout West Virginia. On nearing the Main Overlook, Castle Rock Trail twists its way through boulders in a short but steep ascent to rejoin Canyon Rim Trail. To return to your car, turn left and retrace your steps along Canyon Rim Trail toward the Main Overlook and back to the parking lot.

Tunnel Trail is another well-loved attraction of this park. This short (0.4 mile) trail to the right of the Main Overlook is posted with a sign. The path leads to several natural tunnels in rock outcrops, some of them lighted. Children in particular will enjoy the mysteriousness and the maze-like nature of the dimly lit tunnels.

right lead to overlooks with additional views of the New River Canyon. A short side trail to the North Overlook, marked with a sign, provides a particularly fine view of the river.

At 0.5 mile, Castle Rock trail joins Canyon Rim Trail from the right. At 0.7 mile, the trail emerges onto the road to Turkey Spur Rock. The trail alternately joins and leaves the road three times, finally ending at the road one mile from

14

Twin Falls State Park

Distance: 2.4 miles
Time: 1 hour
Elevation change: 360 feet
Maps: USGS 7½′ Mullens; Park map
Highlight: View

Twin Falls State Park is a 3,776-acre tract of land in southern West Virginia in Wyoming County. The park has much to offer its visitors: a twenty-room lodge, cabins, a restaurant, swimming pool, campground, picnic areas, tennis, and a golf course, as well as hiking trails. In addition, a pioneer farm in the park has been restored. This pioneer farm nestled among the hills in a remote section of the park offers a glimpse into the past at the simplicity (and harshness) of pioneer life.

The park is west of Maber and northwest of Mullens, and it can be reached from WV 97 and WV 54. To reach Cliffside Trail, the hike described here, follow the signs to the campgrounds 4.7 miles from the park entrance. Turn right into Fox Hunter's Point camping area. The trailhead is 0.3 mile from this intersection and across the road from the restrooms. Parking is available at the trailhead.

Cliffside Trail begins as a wide, flat, grassy path along Bear Wallow Ridge. The forest is a mixture of hardwoods and hemlock. Dogwoods are plentiful along the trail edge. Pileated woodpeckers often may be seen flashing among the treetops. Their deep drumming sounds and reverberating throaty cries echo through the forest.

These prehistoric-looking woodpeckers with their distinctive red crests are about the size of a crow. They usually inhabit the upper regions of the forest crown. Unlike any other woodpecker, the pileated strips thick pieces of bark off trees and carves out oblong holes in which to nest. They feast on carpenter ants, beetle larvae, grubs, berries, and wild grapes. A pileated woodpecker hammering on a particular tree is usually a sign that something is wrong with that tree. They do not destroy trees as the result of their foraging, but on the contrary, often seek out and kill the very insects that can destroy a tree, thus actually delaying tree death.

The pileated almost became extinct during the logging era of the early 1900s. Thanks to conservation, it has made a comeback with the regrowth of the oak and hickory forests. Unlike its cousin, the ivory-billed woodpecker, which is possibly extinct, the pileated woodpecker remains for us to enjoy its noisy presence in the forest.

At about 0.3 mile from the trailhead, a side trail intersects from the left. This side trail leads to a shallow dip in the forest floor filled with murky water. This is a bear wallow. The mountain and the side trail were named after such water holes.

In the summer, the large dark black bears may have a hard time keeping cool while they are active. Water-filled hollows such as these are a source of air conditioning for the bears. They wallow in the water, soaking their coats, then they lie quietly and air-dry. The cooling effect of evaporation helps the bears maintain a normal body temperature.

Cliffside Trail at this point continues straight ahead. At approximately 0.7 mile, a clearing appears ahead with a spur path leading to it. Cliffside Trail, however, bends to the left about ninety degrees for about fifty yards, then bends back to the right. The path still follows the ridgetop. The trail enters another clearing about 0.25 mile past the previous clearing, then exits this clearing on the south side. About 150 yards beyond the clearing, the trail forks. Follow the right fork down-

hill through thickets of laurel and rhododendron. Take a right at the next intersection as well. The trail emerges at an overlook about a hundred yards beyond this intersection.

The rocky overlook offers a nice view of Cabin Creek gorge. With the right breeze, the sound of waterfalls may drift up from the valley bottom. Blueberries grow among the rocky ledges. Five-lined skinks sometimes bask on the rocks in the sun.

Less adventurous hikers should retrace their steps from here to their vehicle. The more venturesome can get another view of the gorge by retracing the path from the overlook and taking a right turn at the intersection nearest the overlook. This path takes you through a rhododendron thicket. It is not well maintained and is steep and difficult in places besides. The right fork at the next intersection leads to the second overlook, which offers a

Five-lined skink

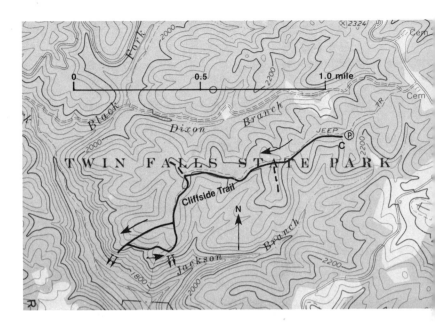

different view of the gorge and another valley to the left.

To regain the original trail, retrace the path to the next intersection, then take a right. This trail is lined with trailing arbutus, galax, and checkerberry. Checkerberry, also known as wintergreen, has an oil of wintergreen odor and taste. Native Americans used its leaves to treat rheumatism. This may have been effective, because a substance similar to aspirin can be extracted from them. The red berries that form in the fall are a principal food of the grouse and wild turkey that inhabit these woods.

Turn right at the next fork in the trail at the top of the ridge, and retrace the path to your vehicle.

A domestic turkey owned by one of the rangers at Twin Falls had been adopted by a flock of wild turkeys when we visited. The ranger didn't seem to mind. He carried a turkey caller in his shirt pocket, and from time to time he would pull it out and utter a turkey call himself.

If you listen very carefully while hiking on Cliffside Trail, you may hear a wild turkey—or maybe even a ranger!

15

Cabwaylingo State Forest: Sleepy Hollow Trail

Distance: 3 miles
Time: 3 hours
Elevation change: 520 feet
Maps: USGS 7½′ Wilsondale, State forest map
Highlights: Seasonal waterfalls, secluded rock outcrops

Cabwaylingo State Forest is nestled in the remote southwestern section of West Virginia. The name Cabwaylingo is formed from interlocking portions of the names of the surrounding counties: Cabell, Wayne, Lincoln, and Mingo. The state forest is 8,123 acres of typical West Virginia hills and valleys. Camping, swimming, fishing, hunting, and hiking are a few of the pleasures found in the forest. Hiking in pleasant solitude can be almost guaranteed, as the trails seem seldom used.

The state forest is easy to find by following the signs off WV 152. The forest entrance is 1.6 miles east of WV 152 on an unnumbered road leading through the forest. Sleepy Hollow Trail starts across the road from the swimming pool that you will find 1.3 miles beyond the entrance sign. Parking is available there.

The trailhead is at the north end of the picnic area across the road from the swimming pool. It follows the west bank of a small stream. The path is badly eroded in spots; sometimes you are actually hiking in a neck-deep ravine. A small seasonal waterfall may be seen along the way up the mountainside. The path follows the drainage until it circles to the right along the contour about forty vertical feet below the ridgetop. Along the ascent, you will see interesting rock formations as well as birds and wildflowers. The forest along the ascending trail is rich with deciduous magnolia trees, with their large umbrella-like leaves.

The path converges with the ridge crest, then circles to the left and follows the ridgetop through drier oak woods. Shortly, the trail dips into a saddle and joins an old jeep trail. Turn right on the jeep trail, following it as it skirts the crest of a knob. The trail then comes out again on a saddle where another jeep trail joins from the left, coming from the top of the knob. Following the ridge, the path continues, soon to intersect with a rough gravel road coming up the mountain and intersecting from the right. Note this gravel road intersection, because about 400 yards beyond this point you must follow the woodland trail that leaves the jeep road on the right side near a shallow drainage ditch. If you cross a culvert and a wide spot in the road, you have gone too far.

The woodland path crosses several jeep tracks that converge in a clearing

Waterfall and rock ledges along
Sleepy Hollow Trail

by a gas well. To regain the woodland trail, follow a small jeep trail that leaves the clearing to the right for about twenty feet. Then the woodland trail veers left over an embankment, crosses another jeep track and descends the mountain.

The path traces a flank of the mountain down a medium grade between two drainages, then bends left around a hollow. Here, a grove of hemlocks and large beeches frames an enchanting scene where a waterfall spills over portions of the rock cliffs that line both sides of the hollow. The path passes over the rock ledges and around the contour of the hollow. Farther down the trail, a spur path leaves from the right and takes you back up underneath the ledges for a spectacular view of the cliffs and the waterfall. In spring, wild irises, clintonia, nodding trillium, and jack-in-the-pulpit are a few of the wildflowers to be seen here.

The path then skirts a small drainage, following the contour and gradually descending through a grove of hemlock seedlings. At the valley bottom, the trail curves right and crosses a wooden bridge over a small stream known as Sleepy Hollow Branch. Once across the bridge, ignore the sharp left spur and take the trail straight ahead, following along a small tributary for about thirty yards, then take a left turn up the slope. Follow the contour along Sleepy Hollow Branch where you will see another rock formation a half mile below the first. The path descends until it finally emerges on Sweetwater Road. Turn right along this road to reach the main state forest road. Turn right again at the junction with the main state forest road to return to your vehicle.

Sleepy Hollow Trail is good for both intermediate and experienced hikers. Portions of the trail are badly eroded, however, and appear to replace the main streambed as the path for spring runoff. The ridgetop is a maze of jeep trails, making the route a bit difficult to follow. Downed trees block the path in a number of places. Despite these drawbacks, though, this hike is well worth taking. The woodland portions of the trail are seldom used, and the scenery has a pristine beauty that you can enjoy in solitude.

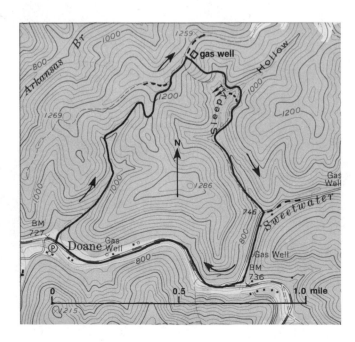

16

Panther State Forest

Distance: 3.1 miles
Time: 2 hours
Elevation change: 1,080 feet
Maps: USGS 7½′ Panther, Iaeger; State Forest map
Highlight: View from lookout tower

In the far southwest section of West Virginia, near the Virgina border, lies remote Panther State Forest. In addition to hiking trails, Panther State Forest has a swimming pool, playgrounds, picnic areas, camping areas, and opportunities for fishing and hunting.

This 7,810-acre tract of land is in the midst of coal mining country. In fact, land within the state forest boundaries currently is being considered for coal mining. Apart from the dust-raising traffic of passing coal trucks, the state forest right now is relatively unaffected by the mining activity that influences the land you pass through as you approach this forest. Because it represents an extensive preservation in an otherwise disturbed area, and because the Panther lookout tower provides a rare view of the hills province, this area is well worth a visit.

Wildflower enthusiasts especially will enjoy visiting, because Bob Beanblossom, the park superintendent, is very knowledgeable and willing to show visitors the special plants encountered here. For instance, this forest is one of only three sites in the country where you will find Japanese loosestrife, a small plant imported from Japan that grows in lawns.

Crossvine, a southern species, grows along the roadside, sending out its impressive orange-red flowers in May and June. Its common name is derived from the fact that a cross-section of the stem reveals a Maltese cross in the center. Another oddity is the planetree, a sycamore relative.

To reach Panther State Forest, follow the signs west off US 52 north of Iaeger. Make a sharp left 1.4 miles from US 52, and follow a small road under an overpass, then across Tug Fork River. Turn right at the fork in the road at 3.8 miles from US 52. Go straight at the fork at the 6.5–mile point. Turn left at 6.9 miles, and left again at 7.9 miles at the curve at Trap Fork Church of God. Take another left at 8.7 miles and you will see the Panther State Forest sign at 8.8 miles from the US 52 turnoff. Drive carefully on these narrow roads, for coal trucks boom along taking up more than half the road and leaving very little room to pass.

Drift Branch Nature Trail is 1.7 miles beyond the forest office and maintenance area. Parking is available on the west side of the road at the trailhead, which is just north of Cowshed Picnic Area. A wooden bridge crossing Panther Creek leads to a map of the trail posted under a map shelter at the trailhead. The path is blazed in red.

This hike is particularly pretty during early May—prime spring wildflower season. Foamflower, bloodroot, wild geranium, trillium, showy orchis, jack-in-the-pulpit, and May apples are but a few of the jewels you will see along the way. The trail begins by paralleling Drift Branch through moist woods of hemlock, rhododendron, beech, birch, cucumbertree, and basswood.

A trail leaves to the right after a quarter of a mile. The nature trail continues straight ahead and climbs fairly steeply. After 0.6 mile, the trail turns away from the stream and goes up a smaller gulch, passing into drier woods of black gum, sourwood, and chestnut oak. Wild turkeys frequenting the area may be heard along with the reverberating drilling and raucous cry of the pileated woodpecker. The trail reaches the crest of a knoll at 0.9 mile and enters a power line swath at 1.1 miles.

After climbing in the clearing of the power line, the trail re-enters the woods at 1.25 miles to wind beneath a small cliff covered with fire pink and tall meadow rue. The trail seems little-used but well-maintained. At 1.4 miles, the trail traverses the side of the mountain along an extremely steep slope, then climbs to

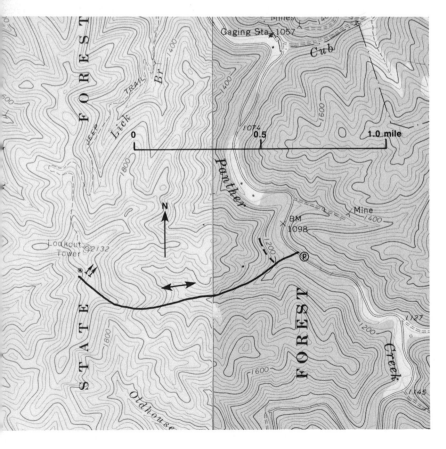

Black snake on a stump

the top of the ridge and intersects with a trail coming in from the left at 1.5 miles. Here, you circle to the right and hike to the fire tower and attendant's cabin at 1.55 miles.

Panther Forest Fire Tower was established in 1940. The elevation at this point is 2,065 feet. The tower is an additional 40 feet high, so if you climb the tower, you will be just over 2,100 feet above sea level. Although the fire tower is not open to the top, you can climb up to the bottom of the shelter portion and enjoy a rare view of the hills province above the trees. To the southeast, the flattened ridgetops are obviously part of a former plateau, while the northwest ridges seem more jumbled and peaked, although most of the tops are about the same height. The dendritic hill and valley formation in this region is the result of streams eroding the softer portions of the plateau.

To return to your vehicle, retrace your steps, taking care not to miss the immediate left turn as you leave the cleared area of the fire tower. Red blazes conspicuously mark this turn as well as the entire trail.

17

Bluestone State Park

Distance: 4.3 miles
Time: 2.5 hours
Elevation change: 840 feet
Maps: USGS 7½' Pipestem; Park map
Highlight: View, self-guided nature trail

Bluestone State Park is situated in one of southern West Virginia's major recreational areas. It is a 2,146-acre recreational facility located along 1,800-acre Bluestone Lake. This park boasts cabins, campsites, a swimming pool, restaurant, rental canoes and motor boats, fishing, and hiking trails, as well as numerous game facilities. In addition, Pipestem State Park golf courses are nearby, and hunting is possible in the adjacent Bluestone Public Hunting and Fishing Area.

The easiest access to Bluestone State Park is from WV 20. Turn west off WV 20 between Hinton and Pipestem State Park on the north side of the bridge crossing the portion of Bluestone Lake where the Bluestone River meets the New River. This turn is well-marked.

Follow signs to the park office, taking a left at the fork in the road 1.6 miles from WV 20. To reach the trailhead, continue 3.7 miles past the park office and restaurant, past Meador Camping Area, and past the swimming area to the entrance of Old Mill Campground. You can park your car in the small pull-off to the left of the fork in the road at the campground entrance. The circuit hike we describe begins with Big Pine Trail, which heads west across the road, about

a hundred feet north of the pull-off.

The narrow footpath climbs steeply through a forest of maple, beech, cherry, and oak with an understory of flowering dogwood. Cucumbertrees are interspersed among the other forest species. In the early spring, its greenish-white flowers, four inches in diameter, stand out among the tiny leaves of spring foliage. The wood of this tree is valued for cabinets and furniture. In the past, carriages often were made from the long straight trunks.

The trail continues climbing and crosses a tiny ravine after about 0.5 mile, then another after 0.6 mile, before leveling out. Faint traces of dull green blazes are visible occasionally on some of the trees along the path. Once level, the trail traverses along below the crest of the ridge. At 0.8 mile you will see several species of large pine trees that are about thirty years old. Some of them are Eastern White Pines. Each year, these trees will add on a whorl of new branches at the top. You can count the number of whorls of branches from the bottom of the tree to the top and get a fairly good estimate of the age of the tree.

The trail descends for a short distance

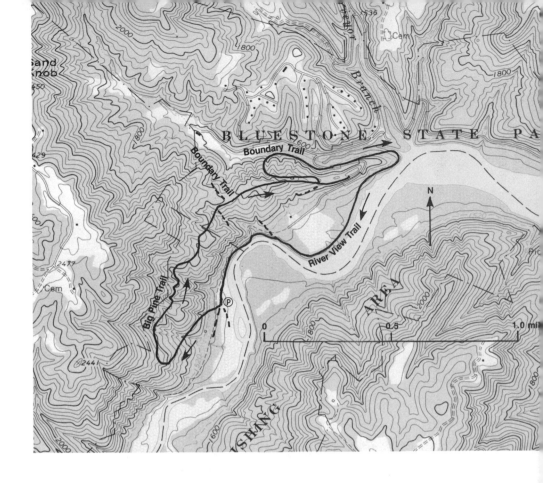

after a mile, levels out, then descends again at 1.1 miles where an old, fallen-in log structure can be seen on the left of the trail. The ridge crest drops to within twenty vertical feet above the path at 1.25 miles, where River View Trail intersects Big Pine Trail on the right. Continue straight along Big Pine Trail through the next intersection at 1.3 miles, where Boundary Trail leaves to the left.

The remnants of a self-guided nature trail begin here. Occasional signs are on some of the trees along the path, to identify the tree and tell the uses of the wood and fruits. At 1.4 miles, for instance, a sign marks a sugar maple, West Virginia's state tree. The wood of this tree is valuable for furniture and flooring, and

the sugar maple of course is the tree from which maple syrup is made.

The trail climbs steeply after this labeled sugar maple to the crest at 1.5 miles, then descends, following the ridge crest, to a power line with views to the north and south at 1.6 miles. At 1.8 miles, another spur of Boundary Trail leaves Big Pine Trail on the left while a spur leading to an overlook continues straight ahead, and Big Pine Trail makes a sharp right turn and descends to the park road. Continue straight to the overlook about 300 yards beyond this intersection.

From the overlook, while resting on a bench, you can see a large expanse of Bluestone Lake. The view of the lake and

Pine needles

a long bridge spanning the water in the distance are nicely framed by the green foliage of nearby trees. This delightful spot is a great place to look down on warblers and other woodland birds flitting about in the tops of the trees below you.

Continue the hike by retracing your steps to the intersection, and take Boundary Trail to the northwest. This trail descends very steeply to the park road. Along the way are a number of labeled trees. At 2.3 miles, one large beech tree has been mislabeled yellow buckeye, so don't believe everything you see in print. Just before it intersects with the park road, the trail levels out and parallels a small stream.

Take a left along the park road for a few paces to pick up River View Trail, which leaves the park road on the east side to follow the stream to the lake shore. The forest along River View Trail is full of moist-woods species such as sycamore, red bud, willow, and joe-pye-weed. The understory in the wettest spots may flash with the red blossoms of cardinal flower from July to September. This flower grows in damp relatively inaccessible places, a factor that has so far prevented its demise from over-picking. Nevertheless, it is not a common flower, and is on the conservation list of flowers to be protected, so it should be enjoyed where you find it and not picked. The brilliant color evokes that of the scarlet robes of the cardinals of the Roman Catholic church, hence its common name.

The stream paralleling the path on the left side plunges over a five-foot ledge at 2.9 miles and over a ten-foot ledge at 3.0 miles. The stream drops into the lake immediately after the large waterfall, and the path bends uphill to the right continuing along the lake. Take a left at the next intersection, following the path as it skirts the lake, sometimes dipping down to it. At 3.3 miles, you will come onto the Meador Campground loop road. Here, turn left and follow the paved road down by the lake.

After passing campsite #3, turn left, crossing a cable into a large field with picnic tables, swings, the pool, and the bathhouse. If you follow the shrubbery line next to the lake, you will intersect a cement walkway connecting the lake with the pool area. Turn left on this cement walkway and follow it to the lake, where it intersects with a fishing trail. Turn right, hiking along the lake to 3.7 miles where the trail divides into three trails.

Here take the leftmost trail and continue along the lake, ignoring all secondary trails leaving to the right, away from the lake. Turn left where the path intersects with a little-used dirt road at 3.8 miles. This trail leads past the tent camping sites to intersect with the main park road at 3.8 miles. Although River View Trail continues across the road, to complete the loop hike you turn left and follow the park road to your vehicle.

18

Chief Logan State Park

Distance: 4.7 miles
Time: 4 hours
Elevation change: 1,200 feet
Maps: USGS 7½' Chapmanville; Park map
Highlight: Spring wildflowers

Chief Logan, a chief of the Mingo Indians of the Upper Ohio Valley, frequented what is now Logan County, West Virginia. He was known for his hospitality, his honesty, his kindness, and his peace-seeking nature. He was trusted and loved by all who met him, even pioneer women and children, until he was sadly tormented and confused by white men. The story, as told by John Hansford is as follows:

"Once, when [Chief Logan] was waiting in the home of a magistrate for a decision on a grievance, he passed the time by playing with the official's daughter who was just learning to walk. The mother remarked that she was unable to buy shoes for the child to help her walk better. When Logan left, the child, spoiled by his attentions, wanted to go with him. It is evidence of his reputation that the mother granted him permission to take the child to his village for the day. Toward nightfall, she began to worry; but just at dusk, Logan, true to his word, came through the woods with the child on his shoulders. On the little girl's feet were neatly crafted moccasins ornamented with beads. He had spent most of the day making them."*

The trust and respect between Logan and the white settlers ended sadly and abruptly when a band of renegade whites killed his only sister and only living brother in the Yellow Creek Massacre in the early 1770s. All his relatives were then dead. Logan, in his grief, blamed one well-known frontiersman, a Colonel Cresap, who was famous for leading reprisal attacks against renegade Indians. In a personal vendetta, Logan waged war on Cresap by attacking white settlements. The renegade Indians gathered inspiration from such a powerful political figure, and they increased their attacks on white settlements, using Logan's campaign to justify them.

Lord Dunmore's War was the result. When white leaders negotiated for peace talks, they knew that without Logan's participation, agreements meant nothing. Lord Dunmore, governor of Virginia, sent Colonel Gibson, a friend of Logan's, to persuade him to attend the talks. Colonel Gibson and Chief Logan met under a large elm tree, and Chief Logan delivered this speech to Colonel Gibson who transmitted it to Lord Dunmore, who read it to the soldiers and Indians at the peace talks.

"I appeal to any white man to say, if

---

*"Who Mourns for Logan?" *Wonderful West Virginia* 34(2):7-10

Hiking along Cliffside Trail

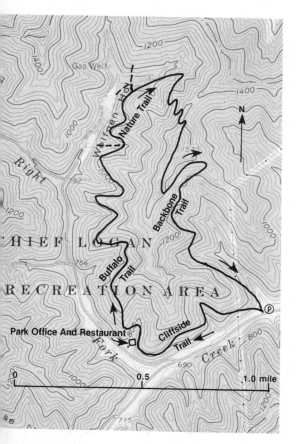

sought it: I have killed many. I have fully glutted my vengeance. For my country I rejoice at the beams of peace. Yet, do not harbor the thought that mine is the joy of fear. Logan never felt fear. He will not turn on his heel to save his life. Who is there to mourn for Logan? Not one."

Chief Logan State Park was named for this tragic figure. It is located in Logan County, about three miles north of the city of Logan. It is 3,305 acres of beautifully reclaimed land with a well-hidden history of disruption. This land was mined extensively for coal. Now the hiking trails wind through remnants of old forests with large trees, and through clean young forests. It is hard to believe that most of this land was an abandoned coal field in the not too distant past.

In a program to increase employment in Logan County, workers were hired to build the park in the 1950s. All the old shacks once used for a mining camp were removed, along with all the abandoned coal tipples and equipment. Buffalo Creek was even rechanneled to improve the use of the land. The old slate piles were removed and used to build the roads and parking lots. Now this scenic park has much to offer in outdoor day recreation ranging from a swimming pool to archery and game courts and hiking trails.

The park entrance is on the northwest side of US 119 and WV 10. Parking for the loop trail described here is at the park headquarters, on the north side of the park road 0.4 mile from the park entrance. The trailhead is at the edge of the forested hillside to the northwest and within view of the park headquarters. The trail forks immediately at the beginning. Take the left fork called Cliffside Trail. The right fork or Backbone Trail will be the return portion of your loop. Cliffside Trail ascends about sixty vertical feet above the park road on Backbone Ridge. It wanders through a forest of

ever he entered Logan's cabin hungry and he gave him not meat: if ever he came cold and naked and he clothed him not. During the course of the last long and bloody war, Logan remained idle in his cabin, an advocate for peace. Such was my love for the whites that my countrymen pointed as they passed and said 'Logan is the friend of white men.' I had even thought to live with you but for the injuries of one man. Colonel Cresap, the last spring in cold blood and unprovoked, murdered all the relatives of Logan: not sparing even his women and children. There runs not a drop of my blood in the veins of any living creature. This called on me for revenge. I have large beeches and buckeyes that obviously were not disturbed by the coal mines.

Jack-in-the-pulpits are found throughout these moist woodlands. The plants were gathered and the corms boiled and eaten by the Indians. Boiling the corms removes the irritating crystals of calcium oxalate. Calcium oxalate crystals cause burning sensations in the mouth, lending a peppery quality, and the Indians taught the settlers to grind the raw corm for use as a pepper substitute. The corm was also used as a counterirritant for sore throats. Calcium oxalate is poisonous in quantities, so do not eat these plants raw as a main course!

The path enters a younger forest of small hardwood trees in about 0.25 mile. The plant species seen here are indicative of the disturbed past of this land. Lousewort, hawkweed, and poison ivy grow among the trees. These plants are typical of open woods, thickets, and clearings.

Cliffside Trail descends after 0.7 mile to traverse above the park restaurant and conference center. The trail then bends right and intersects with Buffalo Trail, which comes up from the road on the left. Continue to the right along Buffalo Trail, up a drainage valley past a stone fireplace on the right side of the trail. Buffalo Trail is a moderately steep trail, but rest benches are provided beside the path. Sweet William, May apple, false Solomon's seal, bloodroot, larkspur, and wild geranium are but a few of the spring wildflowers along the route. The trail wanders in and out of cool moist woods in the watersheds to the drier younger forests on the outer flanks of the ridge.

After 1.4 miles, Buffalo Trail descends to meet part of a selfguided nature trail intersecting from the left. Continue to the right. The path follows the contour of the terrain above a fishing pond in Wolfpen Hollow. Blue-eyed Mary, a plant common to the midwest, grows along the path.

Buffalo Trail intersects with Lakeside Trail and Backbone Trail within 1.9 miles. At this intersection, the nature trail bends off to the left, returning down the east side of Wolfpen Hollow. The Lakeside Trail crosses the lake's feeder creek and circles around to the west side of the lake. Backbone Trail veers off to the right up the mountainside. Follow Backbone Trail.

The hairpin turns of the ascending trail are lined with Dutchman's-breeches, wild ginger, sharp-lobed hepatica, and Virginia bluebells. When these flowers are in blossom in spring, this is an especially lovely hike. Backbone Trail ascends to the crest of Backbone Ridge, then descends slowly on the back side of the ridge. The forest here appears more recently disturbed in spots.

Several nice views are found along the trail, and the flora is different from that along the other trails. The wildflowers represent a mixture of species from rich moist woodlands as well as those in highly disturbed areas. Many of the herbs have lush knee-high foliage; jewelweed, tall meadow rue, masses of false Solomon's seal, celandine poppy, blue cohosh, yellow mandarin, baneberry. The trail drops in elevation, dipping in and out of large watersheds harboring huge cucumber trees and buckeyes. In places the narrow path seems to barely cling to the mountainside. This trail is much less traveled than the other trails in the state park.

After crossing beneath a power line and behind the park headquarters, the trail intersects with Cliffside Trail. Take a left at this intersection and retrace the beginning of the hike to your vehicle.

19

Kanawha State Forest

Distance: 4.7 miles
Time: 3 hours
Elevation change: 960 feet
Maps: USGS 7½' Racine; Park map
Highlights: Spring wildflowers, birds

Kanawha State Forest is the closest outdoor recreation area for residents of West Virginia's state capitol, Charleston. It boasts more than fifty miles of hiking trails, many of them following gated fire roads. The state forest also has an amazing diversity of plants (reportedly over 700 species) and animals (including bobcats) in its 9,000-plus timbered acres. Described here is a circuit hike that takes in two of the many "hollows" in the forest.

Reaching Kanawha State Forest, despite its proximity to Charleston, is no easy task. Take exit 58 off Interstate 64 (the first exit south of the Kanawha River). The exit road intersects with WV 214, which you follow west for 0.6 mile to Oakwood Road. Turn left on Oakwood Road, and follow it 0.6 mile to an intersection. Here, turn left, remaining on Oakwood Road for 0.4 mile. Turn right onto Bridge Road, which becomes Louden Heights Road after 0.4 mile. After 0.2 mile on Louden Heights Road, the route to Kanawha State Forest turns right onto Connell Road. Follow this road 2.3 miles to a sharp bend. Continue following the well-used paved road around the bend and into the little town of Loudendale.

From here, stay on the main road through Loudendale and beyond for 2.4 miles, where a sign marking the entrance to the forest will greet you (at last). On reaching the state forest entrance, follow the main paved road through the forest for 4.2 miles. Just beyond the point where the paved road becomes gravel, you will see a parking lot on the left side of the road for a picnic area. Park your car here.

The trail begins at the far (east) end of the picnic area at the base of Johnson Hollow. Through the picnic area the trail is a paved path, but beyond the last shelter the trail becomes a dirt path. The white-blazed trail follows the bottom of the hollow up a seasonal stream.

At present, this trail is recommended for winter, spring, or early summer travel. In late summer and fall, the trail can be a gauntlet lined by a healthy growth of stinging nettles. Although passage is possible in nettle season (with long pants and a machete), the hike could turn into a close encounter of the torturous kind if you're not careful. Certain plants, including nettles, blackberries, and dogbriar, are the plant equivalent of the biting and stinging insects. The best defense against both kinds of pests probably is to avoid them.

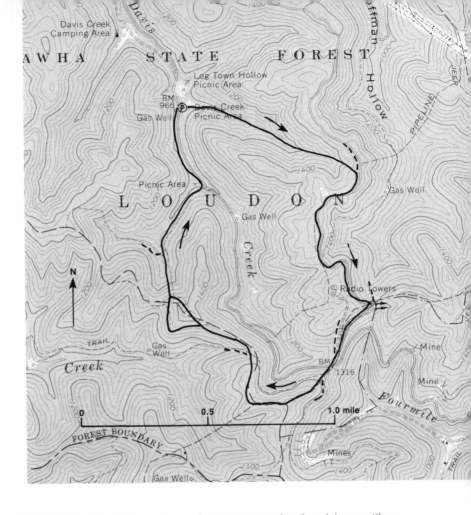

Fortunately, West Virginia is blessed with a comparatively low level of pests, particularly insects. Occasionally you will stumble on swarms of mosquitoes, black flies, deer flies, or no-see-ums, but these occasions are uncommon and tend to occur when you find yourself near a large body of water. Even then, however, if you have ever survived a maddening swarm of Alaskan mosquitoes (the state bird of Alaska) or a dizzying cloud of Adirondack black flies, you will realize how mild the insect climate of West Virginia really is.

Perhaps then the most common pests you will encounter while hiking in West Virginia are the plants. The wise hiker will learn to recognize the vicious nettles, dogbriar, and blackberries. Almost everyone recognizes the long, thorny canes of blackberries. Dogbriar is equally easy to identify with its green, viny stems and prominent sharp thorns. Nettles are not so easy, but one close scrape with a dense patch will encourage your taxonomic interest. Nettles are rather delicate, in contrast to the other two species, although they can grow up to four feet tall. Their leaves occur in pairs along the weak, green stem, and they are coarsely toothed along the margins. The sting comes from contact with tiny hairs that cover the stems and flowers.

One other plant in the pest category

Box turtle

should be mentioned: the famous, or rather infamous, poison ivy. In some ways, poison ivy is the most sinister plant of all. As its ill effects are not felt immediately, the unwary hiker can be thoroughly exposed to rash-producing oil without feeling any immediate pain. Some people are naturally immune to the oil, but those who are susceptible will certainly wish to learn to recognize poison ivy—at a distance.

You have probably heard the saying "leaflets three, let it be," but in fact a few other forest species, such as jack-in-the-pulpit and box-elder, can have three leaflets as well. Without a course in plant systematics, perhaps the best way to dis-tinguish poison ivy from other plants is to recognize that, in addition to having three leaflets, it is usually viny in growth. Realize, however, that the vines may grow over the ground or on shrubs and trees. They may even produce tree-like branches, but you will normally see these branches coming from a vine that winds around a host tree.

Spring wildflowers you may encounter in Johnson Hollow include the showy bloodroot, jack-in-the-pulpit, and wild ginger. The steep-sided hollow is typical of the region. As you ascend, note how the forest and its understory are radically different on the dry south-facing slope as compared to the moist north-facing slope that the trail traverses. Tulip poplars and beeches dominate on the moist slope, while oaks prevail on the drier side of the hollow, reflecting the contrasting habitat preferences of these trees.

As you reach the end of the hollow, the trail ascends steeply, gaining the ridgetop at 0.8 mile. Here, the trail emerges onto a fire road near two white-blazed trees. Turn right (southwest) and follow the road along the flat ridge crest. At 1.6 miles a road intersects from the left, and you bear right, staying on the road you have been following. Nearby, a utility line crosses the road, opening a nice view to the east of a neighboring ridge and valley. At 1.8 miles, the road comes to a gate. Beyond the gate another fire road joins the road you are on from the right, and then you meet the main forest road.

Cross over the main state forest road, and continue on the dirt fire road. Fifty yards beyond this crossing, you reach a fork in the fire road. Bear right at the fork, continuing uphill. At 2.4 miles the fire road forks again and you once again stay right (straight ahead).

At 2.7 miles, the trail skirts to the left of the highest point on the ridge. Here, a glimpse of the surrounding ridges and hollows can be caught through the sparse forest canopy. The forest composition indicates a dry, well-drained site. Sourwood and sassafras are common tree species along with the oaks, and there are dense patches of blueberries and dogbriar in the understory.

At 2.9 miles the fire trail passes below the highest point of the ridge to your right, and at 3.0 miles a gas pipeline crosses the road. At 3.1 miles a small dirt road leaves the main fire trail to the right. You could either follow this trail over a small knob or remain on the fire road. At 3.4 miles these two trails rejoin, and at this junction you meet one spur of Pigeon Roost Trail. The point where the trail meets the fire road is designated by a tree marked with "P1" in white paint. Turn right here onto the white-blazed Pigeon Roost Trail.

Pigeon Roost Trail descends steeply at first, then gradually levels out as you proceed down the hollow. A junction is reached at 3.7 miles with a second spur of Pigeon Roost Trail joining from the left. In the spring this section of the trail is excellent for wildflowers, including bloodroot and jack-in-the-pulpit. At 4.3 miles the trail emerges from the hollow onto the main state forest road. The picnic area, parking lot, and your car, are reached by turning left and following the main road for 0.4 mile.

20

Camp Creek State Forest

Distance: 8 miles
Time: 6 hours
Elevation Change: 840 feet
Maps: USGA 7½' Odd; Forest map
Highlights: Waterfalls

Camp Creek State Forest is in southern West Virginia, about sixteen miles north of Princeton in Mercer County. It encompasses approximately 6,000 remote acres of West Virginia hills, mostly lying west of Camp Creek. According to Kile McCormick, author of *The Story of Mercer County*, settlers named this area for the Indian camps that dotted the creek banks.* Now, instead of Indians, fishermen frequent the streambanks in search of "The Big One." Camp Creek and its tributaries are prime trout fishing streams. In addition to fishing, the state forest has picnicking, playground, and camping facilities, as well as many miles of hiking and hunting trails.

Camp Creek State Forest is reached by taking US 19/21 thirty-one miles south of Beckley or sixteen miles north of Princeton. An all-weather hard-surface road marked by a Camp Creek State Forest sign leads west from US 19/21 1.8 miles to the state forest entrance. The trailhead is located at the far end of the campground 1.3 miles from the state forest entrance. Parking is available at the campground.

The trailhead is at the metal bar gate blocking vehicle access north of the camping area. The path begins as an unmaintained dirt road that winds along the west side of Camp Creek. The stream cascades over a rock ledge beyond the gate. This waterfall was the site of a grist mill in the late 1800s. At 0.7 mile, the dirt road branches. The right branch crosses Bear Creek, while the left branch proceeds up the west bank of Bear Creek.

Follow the left fork uphill. The road had been recently bulldozed as of May 1984. The trail rises above the creekbed, leaving the main drainage after 0.35 mile to head left to follow another smaller drainage valley. Dense stands of rhododendron with scattered hemlocks line the path. After crossing the stream, the path forks. Take the left fork.

Fringed polygala grows here along the trail among the oak and dogwood trees. Fringed polygala blooms from May to July in the mountains. Its name combines two Greek words, *polus*, meaning "much," and *gala*, "milk." In the olden days, these plants and their relatives were eaten by nursing mothers and fed to dairy cattle as well because it was be-

---

*Kile McCormick, The Story of Mercer County (Charleston: Charleston Printing Co., 1957).

Waterfall at the site of the former grist mill

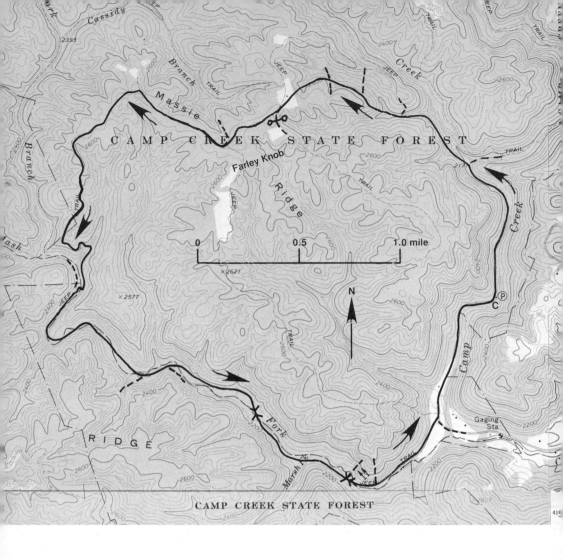

CAMP CREEK STATE FOREST

lieved that they increased milk production.

At the top of the ridge, a road intersects from the right. Proceed straight ahead. The path emerges in a clearing. This clearing and those adjacent to it are managed by the Forest Service to increase habitat diversity and food availability for wildlife. The effect is to increase the variety of birds here. Open-field varieties mingle with deep-forest dwellers. For instance, the woodland call of a black-throated green warbler may be heard

along with the song of the indigo bunting, a field-edge species.

The path passes beyond the clearing to intersect with a road. Continue straight along the level trail, which continues along the northeast side of Farley Knob to another fork in the road. The left fork goes into private property through a gate. Take the right fork. A forest fire has left its mark on the forest here with blackened stumps and scarred tree trunks. The path follows the top of the ridge on a level grade. At the next fork in the trail, take the left branch. The right leads to more wildlife management clearings. The left fork continues along the ridge crest.

In spring time you will see violets, the most common and best known of the wildflowers. Their showy flowers have always been alluring to poets, writers, and romantics. Violets capture our interest for other reasons as well. Many violets have flowers called cleistogamous flowers that never open. These flowers are self-pollinating; they produce copious amounts of seeds, each of which is very similar to the parent plant, for they were formed without another parent. The leaves of violets have been used as a cough remedy and to relieve hoarseness and sore throats. Some people even candy the flowers and make jelly from the petals.

The trail drops below the ridge into deep moist forest. Large pines, hemlocks, trillium, wild geraniums, and sweet William grow in the cove. The trail continues down to the valley bottom where it fords a stream. On the opposite side of the stream, a trail intersects from the right. Continue left down the stream.

Occasionally you may come across wild turkey scratchings. Lucky hikers actually may see the birds firsthand. They are very secretive animals, so most often only small freshly scratched patches of bare ground mark their presence. These large, ground-dwelling birds are strong runners, but even though they are sleeker than their domestic counterparts they are rather poor fliers. They prefer open woodlands where they can find the insects, seeds, and fruits they prefer.

The trail fords the stream many times in this section. A wonderful slide-rock with a swimming hole at the bottom is located between the fifth and sixth ford about 0.7 mile from the first ford. After the seventh ford, a major road comes in from the right. Continue left along the stream. Ignore the next washed-out road to the right. The trail then crosses two bridges, fords a small tributary of the stream, and crosses another bridge. Above the last bridge is a beautiful waterfall.

This portion of the trail along the stream follows the route of a railroad built to haul wood out of the mountains in the early 1900s. The logs were probably sold as staves for barrels to hold whiskey and flour, among other things. Remnants of a railroad trestle may still be found among the rocks next to the falls.

A spur trail leaves on the opposite bank of the stream beside the falls. The main route continues straight along the main road. Take the left fork at the next intersection, where a road leads into the picnic area. The road passes a sign pointing to Farley Branch Trail to the left and to the campground, which is 1.4 miles straight ahead. The road winds through the game facilities, ball field, and picnic tables. Follow the signs back to the campground and your vehicle, taking the left fork at the main park road.

21

Pipestem State Park

Distance: 14.6 miles (10.5 miles if return by tramway)
Time: 1 day
Elevation change: 1,840 feet (760 feet if return by tramway)
Maps: USGS 7½′ Pipestem, Flat Top; Park map
Highlights: Views, cabin, tramway

Pipestem State Park is said to be named for a hollow-stemmed local plant that once was used for making pipe stems. It is well-known both as a family vacation spot and for its convention facilities. This 4,023-acre resort park in the southern part of the state has exciting features for visitors with varied interests.

The park boasts two lodges. One lodge and restaurant is in an enchanting secluded setting along the banks of the Bluestone River deep in the Bluestone Canyon and can only be reached by aerial tramway. The second lodge is modern and convenient to a number of amenities for vacationers. A championship eighteen-hole golf course plus a nine-hole par three course and clubhouse are attractive features for golfers. Indoor and outdoor swimming, tennis matches on lighted tennis courts, and shows at the amphitheater are a few of the entertainment options found here.

For the outdoor-oriented, opportunities for overnight pilgrimages by horseback, cross-country skiing, fishing, hunting, boating, camping, and hiking are all found here or in the nearby Bluestone Public Hunting and Fishing Area. For children, the game courts and playgrounds are added attractions.

From an observation tower near the park entrance on top of Pipestem Knob (elevation 3,100 feet), you can see into West Virginia, Kentucky, Virginia, and Tennessee on a clear day. This is a spectacular vista of land settled predominantly by the Welsh and Scotch Irish. The region abounds with Gordons, Campbells, and Scotts. Some evidence of their traditional heritage is visible in offerings at Pipestem's gift shop. Dulcimers, for instance, are still used by southern mountaineers to accompany their ballads. An occasional brightly colored plaid, fine needlework, and traditional recipes are other clues to the heritage of these people.

The route to Pipestem is well-marked. The entrance is found on the west side of WV 20 between Hinton and Princeton. Parking for Pipestem Knob Lookout Tower is 0.7 mile from the entrance on the right.

The trailhead for the 14.6-mile hike we describe is reached by following the signs to the visitors' center where you can park your car. The top of the Canyon Tramway is at the visitors' center so you can survey the hiking options be-

View from Canyon Tramway

fore you start.

Canyon Rim Trail leaves the lawn of the visitors' center on the northeast side. It is blazed in blue diamonds and descends quite steeply through a young forest of ailanthus, tulip poplar, hickory, and grapevines. The wide dirt path is lined with phlox, golden Alexanders, yarrow, columbine, and bluets. You can hear the Bluestone River below and catch glimpses into the canyon through the trees.

River Trail intersects Canyon Rim Trail at 0.6 mile. Turn left on River Trail and hike down the wide jeep road following the orange diamond blazes. This road also serves as a horse trail. At approximately one mile, River Trail leads left off the dirt jeep track to cross under the tramway. This portion of River Trail is much less worn, yet the turnoff is well-marked by a sign. In the cleared swath beneath the tramway is a nice view into Bluestone Canyon. On the opposite side of the tramway clearing, the path enters a dark hollow with hemlocks bordering a small mountain stream plunging down a ravine.

The vegetation changes abruptly, and here you will find moisture-loving plants such as wild ginger and walking fern. Walking fern is a bizarre prostrate plant that sends out long thin leaves that root at the tip when they come in contact with the ground. Its lines of leaves, end-to-end, typically cascade over moist moss-covered rock ledges.

County Line Trail intersects River Trail from the left at 1.6 miles. Continue straight, following River Trail and the orange diamond blazes. To the right of the trail at 1.7 miles is a small meadow with foundation remains of what may have been an old homestead on the far side. Golden ragwort and wild strawberries abound. The woods are full of chipmunks sounding their warnings as you pass. Deer sign are abundant. In early spring, birds of many types may be enjoyed along the different sections of the trail.

The river becomes much louder and you can see across the valley to a rock outcrop on the opposite bank at 2.5 miles. Several unmarked and inconspicuous trails leave River Trail in its descent to the Bluestone. There is no danger of confusion, however, because River Trail is very well-used and well-blazed. After a horseshoe bend to the right at 3.0 miles, the trail approaches the river and parallels it going downstream for a short distance. Near the bend, a spur trail leads upriver to a small overlook.

Continue along River Trail, following the orange blazes, to the ford across the Bluestone. Do not attempt to cross the river in high water. Normal water depth is eighteen inches. Even at that depth it is nice to have a walking stick for support, as the flow is surprisingly strong.

On the opposite side of the river, the trail leads into a small open area. A narrow trail leads out of the cleared area to the left heading upriver, and another leads across the clearing toward the rock outcrop. Follow the latter toward the cliffs to intersect with a dirt road, which leads to the lodge in the canyon. Turn right on the dirt road, and follow it to the lodge and picnic area by the river at 4.1 miles.

River Trail leaves the picnic area on the east side of the lodge, leading into the woods beside a sign. This portion of the hike is much less traveled. Along the banks of the path, one-flowered cancer root may be seen in the spring. This plant consists of a single, downy pale violet flower on the top of a sticky pale leafless stem. It is parasitic on the roots of some plants.

At 4.7 miles you pass a cable system for taking items across the river and a building that looks like a weather monitoring station. The path continues paralleling the river to a fork at 5.1 miles where the

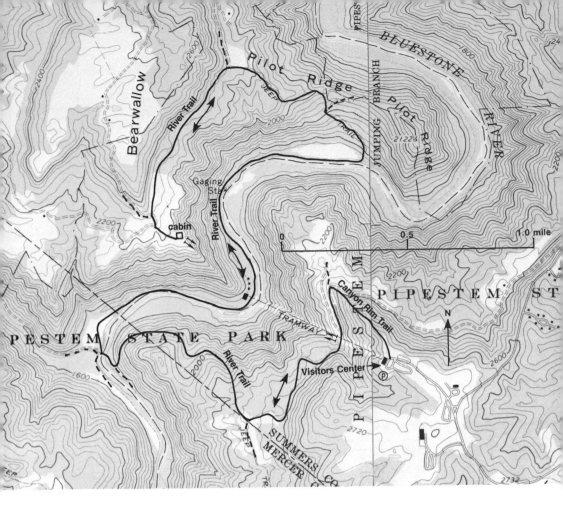

muckiness of the original path has led to the formation of an alternate path (which is now just as mucky). These paths reconnect at 5.2 miles where the trail curves to the left away from the river. At this curve, a smaller trail follows the river downstream. Be sure to turn left following the orange blazes.

River Trail ascends Pilot Ridge at a moderate grade circling left at 5.5 miles to enter an almost pure white oak forest. At 5.75 miles, the track curves to the right and at 5.8 an old logging road leaves to the right while the main trail curves to the left and continues up Pilot

Ridge to Bearwallow Ridge. A hemlock, beech, and maple forest is encountered at the higher elevations at 6.3 miles.

At 6.6 miles, an unmarked trail joins from the right. Here, River Trail begins to traverse Bearwallow Ridge along an almost level grade. Several very small trails intersect River Trail along the way, but there is no danger of becoming confused. River Trail is well-blazed and is the most obvious path. The trail enters smaller woods, then an overgrown meadow where Bearwallow Ridge descends to the meadow at 7.2 miles. At 7.3 miles the path descends to intersect with a dirt road. Go left at this intersection, following the path into an open field.

A restored log cabin sits on the far side of this field on the rounded edge of the canyon overlooking the Bluestone. From here, you can view the visitors' center and main lodge across the canyon. Views of the surrounding countryside are excellent. In early spring, golden-winged warblers tease you from the tops of the scattered trees. This cabin is used as an overnight campsite by horseback riders. It is a wonderful spot to enjoy the night under the stars around a campfire.

To return, retrace your steps to the lodge on the banks of the Bluestone (10.5 miles total distance from the trailhead). Here you can decide whether you wish to hike the remaining 4.1 miles back to the visitors' center and your car, or take the Canyon Tramway. The 6,600 foot tramway will take you painlessly up the canyon side to your car for a modest fee. If you decide to celebrate by eating in the lodge restaurant, the tramway ride is free. Dogs and babies are allowed on the tramway free of charge in any case.

Northern Mountain Province

22

Gaudineer Scenic Area

Distance: 0.6 mile
Time: 1/2 hour
Elevation change: 180 feet
Maps: USGS 7½′ Durbin, Wildell
Highlights: Virgin forest

Gaudineer Knob and Gaudineer Scenic Area are named for Don Gaudineer, a United States Forest Ranger of the Greenbrier District who died while saving others from a forest fire. Gaudineer Scenic Area is one of West Virginia's "high" spots for two reasons. First, the elevation is over 4,000 feet above sea level, and second, it is one of the few easily accessible stands of virgin forest left in West Virginia. The forest here, however, does not resemble descriptions of the spruce forests of pre-lumbering days when pure stands of spruce grew so thickly that light could not penetrate the branches to the ground. This enchanting woodland consists of a mixture of immense birch, beech, and spruce trees.

As you walk among the trees, the forest appears to be literally falling apart. Huge trunks and limbs of dead giants litter the ground. The young trees are often scarred by the battering they receive when a neighboring behemoth falls. Huge gaps in the canopy exist above the skeletons of recently fallen trees.

The visitor quite understandably can come away with conflicting impressions. On the one hand, the forest community

Ian McGraw hiking along trail

bespeaks a peaceful, unchanging, timelessness. It has existed for multitudes of years just as it is now, and it may exist in this same state far into the future. On the other hand, individual tree specimens speak of the brevity and hardships of life. A single tree shows the battle scars gained in its struggle against the elements, against disease, and against the competition of other trees in its fight for survival. Very few, and only the strongest, or luckiest of the young trees survive to stand among the giants.

Gaudineer Scenic Area is located on Shavers Mountain near the Randolph-Pocahontas County line. The West Fork of the Greenbrier River lies in the valley to the east, and the Shavers Fork River lies in the valley to the west. The easiest access is from US 250 west of Durbin. At the top of Back Allegheny Mountain, near the highest point between Durbin and Cheat Bridge, turn north on Forest Service Road 27. The road forks 1.8 miles north of US 250. The left fork takes you to a picnic area. The right fork takes you to the Scenic Area, which is about one mile beyond the fork. There you will find a parking lot on the east side of FS 27.

Virgin Spruce Trail, a loop trail, winds

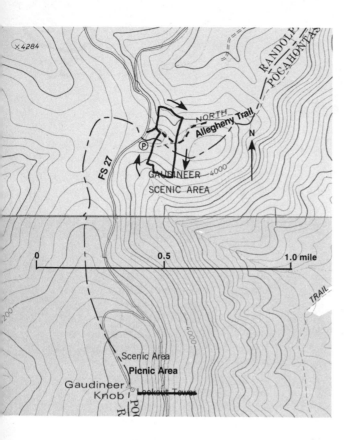

for about 0.6 mile through the scenic area. It is blazed in yellow and is easily followed. Rest benches are provided at intervals beside the path. Interpretive signs point to highlights along the way. This trail and the alternative 0.35-mile loop short cut are ideal trails for a short outing with the entire family.

Virgin Spruce Trail starts on the northeast side of the parking lot. Shortly after you enter the woods, the trail forks to form the loop. Take the left fork. The ancient canopy of the virgin forest has an understory of ferns, wood sorrel, and thick mosses. The forest floor is littered with humps formed by boulders and moss-covered, decaying logs. Newly fallen limbs and leaves lie scattered over the mosses and wood sorrel. The litter,

which lends a rough, unkempt appearance to the forest floor, is important to the maintenance of a rich soil.

After hiking about 0.3 mile, you will encounter a short footbridge across a rivulet. The bridge is made from one large log split in half. Just beyond this is another similar bridge. The logs in these bridges are obviously those split from one of the fallen giants. Some of the standing monarchs are over ten feet around at the base and over one hundred feet tall.

Disease is common among the forest species. Beech bark disease is one of the most obvious. The white waxy spots so common on the beech trees are caused by the beech scale. This insect secretes the white waxy substance to protect itself from adversity while it drills its mouthparts through the thin beech bark to suck sugars and nutrients from the tree. The insects alone will not kill a tree, but holes left by the insects are a perfect route for establishment of a fungal infection that stops the flow of sap. If a tree becomes highly infested with the beech scale, and consequently heavily infected by the fungus, it will die. Another insect-caused disease is very obvious. At least one of the huge birch trees you pass along the path has a large abnormal growth on its side. These growths, which are called burls, actually are prized for furniture and bowls because of the intricate rounded swirls they make in the wood grain.

The path forks at about 0.3 mile. The right fork leads straight back to the parking lot. The left fork continues through the forest to intersect very shortly with Allegheny Trail, which is being planned and developed by the West Virginia Scenic Trails Association. Eventually, the trail will stretch 227 miles, from the Mason-Dixon Line in Preston County, south to the Appalachian Trail in Monroe County. Take the right fork at the Allegheny Trail intersection, which leads to the point where the short cut rejoins this longer loop trail at 0.6 mile. At this intersection, turn left, following the path back to the parking lot.

23

Sinks of Gandy

Distance: 2 miles
Time: 2 hours
Elevation change: 65 feet
Maps: USGS 7½' Sinks of Gandy
Highlight: Sinks

The Sinks of Gandy is unmistakably one of West Virginia's most bizarre natural wonders. In a remote southeast section of Randolph County, Gandy Creek wanders complacently and slowly through wet meadows filled with grazing cattle, then suddenly disappears into a gaping hole in the limestone flank of Yokum Knob to reappear 0.8 mile later on the other side of the knob. This odd formation has not been developed commercially, but belongs to some very generous people who allow the public access as long as visitors respect the property and close the gates.

It is possible to follow Gandy Creek through the mountain as it makes its way in the darkness, to emerge on the other side. The tunnel carved by Gandy Creek is wide enough and high enough not to require crawling or special equipment. The only requirements for hiking through the mountain are two good strong flashlights per person (one for back-up), old clothes that you don't mind getting muddy, shoes with good traction that you don't mind getting wet, and common sense. In addition (as with all hikes), someone not hiking the cave with you should be aware of where you are in case you get into trouble.

The best time to experience the thrill of hiking the Sinks of Gandy is during the warm, dry summer months when the dangers of cold temperatures and flooding are lowest.

The Sinks of Gandy is reached by turning west off WV 28/US 33 onto Briery Gap Run Road, between Judy Gap and Riverton. This road leads past Spruce Knob and Spruce Knob Lake. Following the signs for Spruce Knob Lake, turn left at the fork in the road 1.9 miles west of WV 28/US 33. The paved road turns to gravel at 2.6 miles from the main highway. Continue straight on FS 112 at the fork at 10.1 miles. At an intersection at 16.1 miles, take the right, still following signs to Spruce Knob Lake (Woodlands Institute is to the left). Take the leftmost road continuing past the campground at 16.8 miles. Make a sharp left turn at the next intersection, at 19.3 miles.

Continue straight ahead, ignoring the sharp right one-half mile beyond the sharp left turn. The road curves sharply to the right at some cabins after 1.3 miles. The last section of the loop trail we describe exits from the meadow on the right side of the road and follows the road 0.3 mile west from this curve to the trailhead. It is possible to park a pickup car here if you wish to make a shuttle instead of a loop hike. Otherwise, continue driving 0.3 mile farther to the next sharp right curve in the road, and park your car in the wide pull-off to the left of this hillside curve.

The trailhead is the wooden gate on the southwest side of the bend in the road, and it is completely unmarked. A couple of large boulders just inside the gate make an ideal lunch spot before beginning the hike. After closing the gate behind you, walk down the sloping field heading west in the direction of the barn on the far hillside. To your left in the valley is a spruce stand and to the right is a hillside, grazed by cattle. Continue down the hillside parallel to the forest edge.

After hiking through the meadow for 0.4 mile, you will come upon Gandy Creek, where looking north, downstream, you will see the amber water bubbling merrily into a wide gaping hole in the hillside. This is the site of much unsavory history. Many a cold-blooded killing has occurred here because it is so easy to conceal the evidence of murder by throwing the victim into the waters of Gandy Creek, there to be swallowed up by the blackness and forgotten. Horse thieves, highwaymen, and cattle rustlers have made this their meeting place. During the Civil War, a bunch of pro-Union guerillas used this as their hideout and harassed and killed sympathizers of the Confederacy. Mountain men sympathetic to the Confederacy were also known to attack Yankees clothed in Union blue, strip them of their valuables and equipment, and toss their bodies into the Sinks.

Even now, it is too easy to imagine the horrors possible in this eerie setting, especially when you are wandering in the black interior of the hillside with only your flashlight and your companions to allevi-

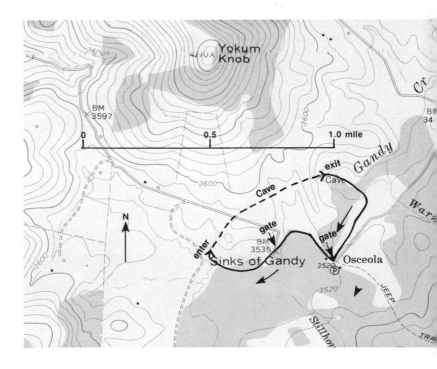

ate your fears. Flashlights play tricks with fertile imaginations, painting monstrous shadow figures on the cave walls and transforming submerged boulders into unrecognizable creatures. Steady nerves and a love for adventure are assets to hikers enveloped in the darkness of the mountain.

Continue the hike by taking the plunge, getting your feet wet, and following Gandy Creek into the cave. The creek is easy to follow. Arrows pointing back the way you came have been painted on the walls. Following the main channel, you cannot go wrong until you near the end, 0.8 mile from the entrance. Here the main channel runs down a long passageway with a very narrow ledge on the right side. Do not go down the passageway on the ledge, but instead turn right following the path up through a narrow passageway into a large room that ends in a tunnel leading to daylight on the other side of the mountain.

If you pass this right turn by mistake, you will end up on the banks of a large deep pool at the end of the narrow passageway. There is no way out from here; you must retrace your steps to the beginning of the passageway where you will find the large room by turning east, or left, following the arrows painted on the walls. If this turn still eludes you, do not panic; you can always retrace your steps to the entrance.

The large mouth of the cave is surrounded by evergreens and ferns. The path emerges into an open meadow. Here, you can stop and rest on the grassy banks of Gandy Creek, enjoying the daylight, munching a snack, washing off mud, and reliving your trip. To continue, turn right and follow the cowpath paralleling the tree line to the left and the hill crest to the right for 0.2 mile to the far end of the meadow. You will come to an open forest where the path crosses a very small creek.

The trail then emerges into another open meadow, where you bear right following a cowpath so that on your left is the gravel road leading to your car, and to the right is a line of trees. The path intersects with the road at a gate at the sharp right bend with the cabins mentioned earlier as a possible parking spot for a shuttle. Remember to close the gate behind you.

To return to the trailhead, turn right and follow the road 0.3 mile west to the second sharp right bend in the road.

Blackwater Falls State Park

Distance: 3.3 miles
Time: 2 hours
Elevation change: 280 feet
Maps: USGS 7½' Blackwater Falls, Mozark Mountain; Park
  map
Highlights: Views, waterfall, bog

Blackwater Falls State Park, although small (1,688 acres), is one of the true gems in the West Virginia state park system. Centered around the canyon of the Blackwater River, the park is known for its breathtaking scenery in all seasons. In the hot days of summer, visitors enjoy temperatures that are often ten degrees cooler than those in the surrounding lowlands. When it rains, the park's streams and rivers swell, and the water falls roar. In winter, deep snow transforms the park into a playground for cross-country skiers and other visitors.

To reach the park, watch for a large state park sign between the small towns of Thomas and Davis, on WV 32, where the road to the park turns west. On reaching the entrance to the park, follow signs to the lodge to reach the trailhead. At a junction 0.3 mile past the park entrance, turn left and stay on this road for 1.6 miles to the lodge parking lot.

The loop trail described here follows sections of four named trails. Part of one trail (Red Spruce Riding Trail) follows a horseback riding route, and it is closed while horses are on the trail. Check at the stable or with a park ranger to find out when the trail is available to hikers. In summer, the trail usually is open to hikers

in the early morning, late afternoon, and evening. In other seasons the stable is closed, and hikers may use the trail any time.

The hike begins on Falls View Trail. Reach the trailhead by walking forty yards past the turnoff to the lodge parking lot on the main park road. The trailhead is marked by a sign and the trail by green blazes. It begins with a gradual ascent in a dense hemlock and birch forest and then bends left. At about 0.5 mile a clearing may be seen to the right through the trees, with a side trail leading into the clearing. Watch for the green blazes, and stay left at this point. You'll notice the trail becomes rockier after this.

At 0.8 mile the trail emerges onto a spur road off the main park road. Follow this road to the right toward the riding stables. Just beyond the stable itself, follow Red Spruce Riding Trail, a graveled and occasionally muddy route. At 1.3 miles the trail crosses a power line right-of-way. The loop hike could be short-circuited here by following a small trail to the right under the power line back to the lodge parking lot. Red Spruce Riding Trail continues straight ahead. At 1.4 miles a trail called "Stemwinder Grade" intersects from the left. At 1.6 miles the trail crosses Shay Run, a small tributary of the Blackwater River.

The brownish-orange color of the water in Shay Run is striking. Why is there a brown stream in a seemingly pristine forest? In more populated areas of the country, you would probably assume that the stream is polluted. The answer, however, lies in natural processes occurring farther upstream. Many of the high-elevation streams in West Virginia originate in flat, naturally boggy areas. Here, the slow-moving water leaches organic chemicals from plant materials, and it takes on the color of these chemicals. Adjacent to Shay Run is one small sphagnum bog that undoubtedly contributes to the coloration of Shay Run. The Blackwater River, which drains the flat and somewhat boggy expanse of Cana-

an Valley, derives its name from the tea-colored water that is produced in such situations.

High-elevation bogs are interesting in a number of ways. They are unique in their species composition; rushes, sedges, and a prickly dwarf raspberry are the dominant plants, along with sphagnum moss. The bogs resemble miniature versions of the well-known Cranberry Glades, occurring in small patches in many areas of the high-elevation Appalachians. In a way, for plants that can survive only in such wetlands, these patches are "islands," for the land between wetlands is essentially an uninhabitable "sea" of forest. Despite their contribution to water coloration, such bogs seem to be capable of improving water quality in some ways. For example,

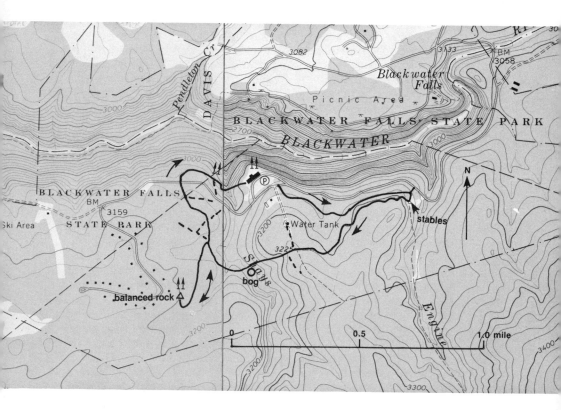

very acidic water from coal mine drainage apparently becomes more neutral as it circulates through a wetland.

Another unusual feature of such habitats is that many bog plants produce copious amounts of seeds, yet actual establishment of seedlings seems rare in undisturbed bogs. The production of seeds may not be in vain, however, because in many species the seeds can remain alive within the soil for long periods, creating a living "seed bank." Eventual disturbance of the wetland may bring these seeds to the surface, allowing germination to occur precisely when establishment (within the disturbed area) is possible. Although seed banks are found in a number of plant communities, they tend to be very large in wetlands. In fact, a sphagnum bog less than ten miles from Blackwater Falls has been found to contain the largest natural seed bank yet discovered in the world. A conservative estimate places the seed bank size at more than five billion seeds in the small wetland—a number exceeding the number of humans on the entire earth.

Red Spruce Riding Trail passes another small bog just past the bridge over Shay Run. At 1.8 miles the trail comes to a junction and another stream. Balanced Rock Trail crosses the riding trail here. For a short side trip to Balanced Rock and a view of the surrounding countryside, turn left at this junction. The trail is blazed in orange and ascends steadily. At 1.9 miles an unmarked trail intersects from the left. At 2.0 miles the trail levels out and then crosses under a power line. Just beyond the power line a trail to the right leads to the cabin area.

The trail to Balanced Rock continues straight, leading through a dense rhododendron thicket. At 2.1 miles the trail reaches a sign pointing to the right toward Balanced Rock. A wooden ladder leads to the top of the rock where a view toward the canyon and lodge can be enjoyed. Balanced Rock is about twenty feet high and is indeed perched atop another rock.

To continue with the circuit hike, retrace your steps to the junction with Red Spruce Riding Trail (2.4 miles), cross over the stream to your left, and then turn right to continue down Balanced Rock Trail. At 2.6 miles you cross a fire trail, and just beyond it Balanced Rock Trail bends left, still marked with orange blazes. Shay Trace Trail joins Balanced Rock Trail from the right at 2.7 miles. While you are still on Balanced Rock Trail, at 2.8 miles you reach an intersection with the paved park road. On the far side of the road, opposite Balanced Rock Trail, follow Elakala Trail into a hardwood and hemlock forest along a ridge.

At 3.0 miles you reach a trail junction and take the left fork. A short spur trail to the left near the junction takes you to an overlook that provides an excellent view of Blackwater River Canyon, rock outcrops on the far side of the canyon, and the lodge 0.2 mile away on the south rim. At 3.1 miles the trail approaches Elakala Falls, where Shay Run begins its steep plunge into the canyon. Depending on recent rainfall, the falls can be a delicate shower or a heavy deluge. In either case, Elakala Trail provides a beautiful vantage point. You can even view the falls from above as the bridge over Shay Run spans the top of the waterfall.

At 3.3 miles the trail emerges into the clearing beside the lodge and the lot where your car is parked. The overlook north of the lodge provides another superb look at the canyon of the Blackwater River.

Canaan Valley State Park: Weiss and Bald Knob Trails

Distance: 3.4 miles
Time: 2 1/2 Hours
Elevation change: 960 feet
Maps: USGS 7½' Laneville, Blackwater Falls; Park map
Highlights: View, spruce and fir forest, chair lift

Weiss and Bald Knobs are located in the southeast corner of Canaan Valley State Park. The trail to Bald Knob will give you a beautiful view of Canaan Valley from an elevation of 4,308 feet. This trail is perfect for those who love to enjoy the scenery of the highlands but who would rather not struggle 960 vertical feet from the parking lot to the top to gain the perspective. In winter the trail could be enjoyed by advanced cross-country skiers. The route is designed around a chairlift that operates year-round and will take you from an elevation of 3,500 feet to an elevation of 4,200 feet.

To reach the trailhead, take WV 32 ten miles south of Davis or nine miles north of Harman. Turn east off WV 32 following the signs to the ski area of Canaan Valley State Park. The ski area is located on Weiss Knob, a portion of Cabin Mountain. Follow this road for about half a mile to either of two parking lots, one below the maintenance buildings and the other just below the ski lifts.

If you wish to take the chairlift to the top of Weiss Knob, tickets must be purchased in the Valley Haus, which is the building right below the chairlifts. Tickets were $3.00 for a round trip chairlift ride in 1985, although on this hike you use the ticket only one way. The chairlift base is considered the trailhead whether you ride the chairlift or hike underneath it.

If you feel energetic, or frugal, you may walk to the top of the chairlift and meet your less energetic companions at the top before continuing on to Bald Knob. Hiking is allowed under the chairlifts during nonski season. Begin hiking up the mountain under the yellow chairlift. The steep trail consists of a mown swath of grasses and daisies in the summertime. To wintertime skiers it is known as Valley Vista Run. After you hike about 0.3 mile, the view becomes very nice as you turn around and look back down into Canaan Valley. At about 0.4 mile, you reach the mid-station of the yellow chair. After about half a mile the trail splits. Continue straight, following the yellow chairlift and ignoring the ski slope to the right. You will soon come to an intersection just before the end of the yellow chairlift. Take a left at this intersection and follow the silver chairlift to the top, 0.75 mile from the trailhead. From this summit, one of several exquisite views of Canaan Valley can be enjoyed.

At the top of the adjacent black chairlift

McGraws on Bald Knob

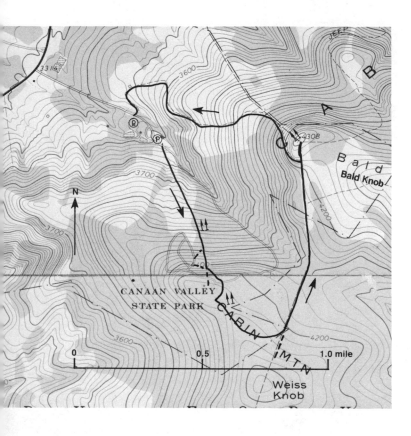

is a large clearing with outhouses on the right as you exit the lift. The head of Weiss Knob Trail is found opposite the outhouses. This trail, which leads to the base of Bald Knob, is clearly marked with a sign. The trail is a narrow, rocky footpath through a beautiful spruce and fir forest. In the summer, wood sorrel and lush mosses form a delicate carpet under the forest canopy. Black-throated blue warblers, juncos, hermit thrushes, and ravens may be heard as you pass through these woods.

Spruce and fir trees are commonly more northern species, but here they have come to reside in West Virginia. This forest is only a reminder of what the entire Canaan Valley was like in the past. Before the days of lumbering, these

forests were so thick that light could not penetrate to the ground; as a consequence very few plants grew beneath the trees.

The fact that balsam fir is found growing on this mountaintop means that the forest floor is damp most of the time. Balsam fir typically grows in swamps and along streams. There are only a few places in the state where balsam fir occurs naturally, and the Canaan area is by far the most extensive site. These trees are often called blister pine, although they are not true pines. If you look closely at the bark, you will notice bumps interrupting the smoothness. These bumps cover little pockets that will ooze a sweet-smelling extremely sticky resin if you break the "blister" with your thumbnail.

The trail intersects with a gas line clearing at 1.1 miles. Turn left and hike for about thirty yards, where you follow the trail to the left back into the woods. Within another hundred yards, the trail re-enters the clearing. The trail then continues through the center of the clearing. Small spruce trees are beginning to invade the open area, which is currently covered with grasses, blueberries, and blackberries. Bald Knob can be seen straight ahead as you look down the clearing. The flag spruce, whose branches grow only on the leeward side of the tree, testify to the harsh climate they encounter on Bald Knob.

Weiss Knob Trail ends when it intersects with Bald Knob Trail at 1.8 miles. To reach the summit of Bald Knob, go straight ahead; the left turn is the return portion of the hike. The trail to the summit is a short (0.2 mile) but steep climb. The knob is treeless. Only hardy ground-hugging plants inhabit the thin, rocky soils of the summit. From the top, a most spectacular view of Canaan Valley can be seen.

Canaan Valley (pronounced ca-nane') is a basin 3,200 feet in elevation surrounded by mountains rising over 4,000 feet. Bald and Weiss Knobs are on the east side of the valley, which is divided by the Blackwater River. This tributary of the Cheat River winds slowly through the flatlands of the valley floor. Alders, balsam fir, and quaking aspens border the banks. Within Canaan Valley is the most extensive wetland in the state. Some of the glades harbor cranberries, creeping snowberry, purple-fringed orchis, wild lilies, and gentians, to name just a few of the wildflowers. Above the valley, ravens and an occasional goshawk soar on the updrafts.

The return route involves retracing your steps down the steep knob to the junction of Bald Knob Trail and Weiss Knob Trail. Turn right on Bald Knob Trail, which lies below the summit cliffs. It descends steadily from Bald Knob, wandering in and out of strips of pasture and forest until it intersects with a gravel road at 3.2 miles. Turn right on the gravel road and follow it to its junction with the main park road to the ski area at 3.4 miles. At this point you encounter a cable across the gravel road blocking vehicle access and a sign for Bald Knob Trail. Turn left on the main park road, and hike the short distance to your car in the nearby parking lots.

Dolly Sods Wilderness Area: Red Creek

Distance: 6.3 miles
Time: 5 1/2 hours
Elevation change: 1,240 feet
Maps: USGS 7½' Blackbird Knob, Laneville, Hopeville,
Blackwater Falls; *Hiking Guide to Monongahela National Forest and Vicinity*
Highlights: Beaver ponds, scattered representatives of boreal flora

Dolly Sods is a 32,000-acre Wilderness Area in the highlands of northeastern West Virginia. The area is well known for its sphagnum bogs, open meadows, heath barrens and scattered spruce. The landscape bears a resemblance to areas much farther north.

Dolly Sods is named for the Hessian soldier, Johann Dahle, who decided to stay in the United States after the Revolutionary War and bought land in this area. His name has been anglicized to John Dolly. Sods is an Old English word meaning meadows or grasslands. The real "Dolly Sods" is only about a square mile of grassland that refers to the original Dolly property. The name now applies to the entire Wilderness Area.

Dolly Sods is a popular destination for people seeking the solitude and pristine beauty of wilderness. Several hikes or backpack trips are possible on marked trails within the wilderness boundary. To reach the trailhead of the hike we describe, take the Laneville Road (WV 45) from WV 32 just south of Canaan Valley State Park. The Laneville Road, although paved and not heavily traveled, is narrow and steep, so drive carefully, especially in bad weather. After seven

miles you will come to a bridge across Red Creek. Cross the bridge and park your car near the wildlife manager's cabin.

The trail begins behind the cabin on the left bank of Red Creek and is called Red Creek Trail. You may have noticed a "high water" route on the right bank of Red Creek before you crossed the bridge. If heavy rains or melting snow have turned Red Creek into a raging river, you will want to save the hike we describe for drier weather, or only take part of the hike now. Our route will cross Red Creek (without the aid of a bridge) and eventually bring you back via the high water route.

Red Creek Trail begins by following an abandoned railroad grade through mixed hardwood forest and stands of large rhododendrons. The trail passes through and near some clearings on the flood plain. About half a mile above the cabin in one such clearing you reach a location marker showing that Little Stonecoal Trail leaves Red Creek Trail to the left. Stay on Red Creek Trail, which remains on the flat flood plain of Red Creek. In the

Wild raisin

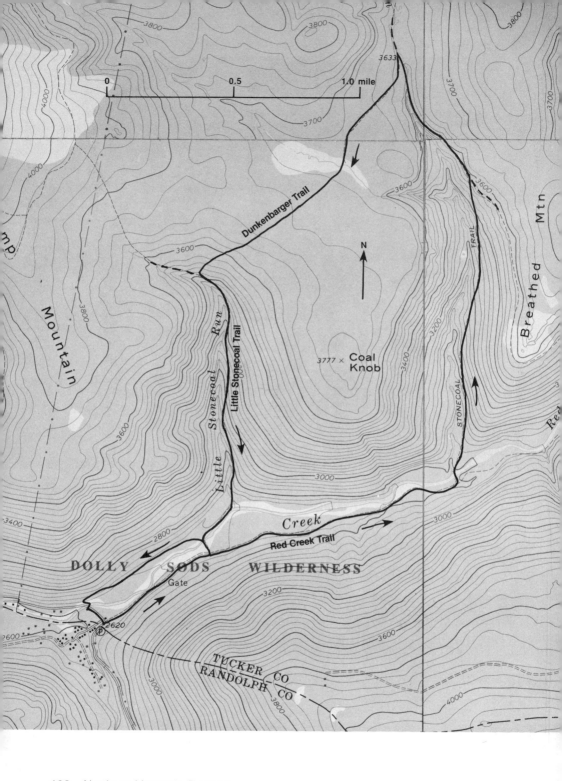

0   0.5   1.0 mile

N

3800

3633

3700

3700

Dunkenbarger Trail

3600

Breathed Mtn

Mountain

Little Stonecoal Run

Little Stonecoal Trail

3777 × Coal
Knob

STONECOAL TRAIL

Creek

Red Creek Trail

DOLLY SODS WILDERNESS

Gate

2620

TUCKER CO
RANDOLPH CO

next mile you may encounter excellent bird watching in the lush streamside vegetation. As you are at a fairly high-elevation (2,700 feet), you may hear or see birds that are common farther north, such as the hermit thrush and veery. The summer ranges of these birds extend south only at high elevations in the Appalachians, where climatic conditions resemble those in the northern United States and Canada.

Evidence of recent beaver activity also may be encountered. At the time of this writing the trail was flooded in one place by a new beaver dam. Beaver activity, however, is a transient aspect of high-elevation streams in West Virginia. Soon this dam will be abandoned in favor of another location, perhaps farther upstream.

At about 1.5 miles from the trailhead, the trail intersects a small logging road coming in from the right. Here, another location marker shows Big Stonecoal Trail coming in from the left across Red Creek. Take Big Stonecoal Trail, boulder-hopping across the creek, or if necessary wading through the shallow areas, to reach the other side. In high water it is dangerous to attempt this crossing.

After crossing Red Creek you will be paralleling Big Stonecoal Creek, occasionally hiking on another old railroad grade. The trail ascends at a moderate grade above the valley bottom, reaching a pair of switchbacks as it nears the ridgetop below some rock outcrops. At nearly 1.5 miles from the Red Creek crossing (three miles from the trailhead), Rocky Point Trail comes into Big Stonecoal Trail from the right. A half-mile from here, bear left at the sign pointing to the Dunkenbarger Trail. Soon you reach a nice waterfall on the left side of the trail. The trail emerges into an open forest with low shrubs such as blueberries and huckleberries among scattered spruce trees. The trail crosses Big Stonecoal Creek, and about a hundred yards beyond the creek you reach the Dunkenbarger Trail, which leaves Big Stonecoal Trail to the left through a spruce forest.

Take the Dunkenbarger Trail blazed with red and blue paint marks. This trail passes near boggy and dry clearings in the forest, both containing northern plant and animal species. After walking three-quarters of a mile from Big Stonecoal Creek, you reach Dunkenbarger Run. Cross Dunkenbarger Run straight ahead and then go upstream twenty yards before following the trail to the left into the woods. Several small paths leave the main trail in this area. You continue on the level through a beautiful forest of deciduous trees, red spruce, and laurel before descending to Little Stonecoal Trail. Turn left (south) on Little Stonecoal Trail, following Little Stonecoal Run down a moderate pitch toward the valley of Red Creek. Near the valley bottom, the trail crosses Little Stonecoal Run and intersects with the high water route.

You could return to your car by recrossing Red Creek here and rejoining Red Creek Trail on the far side, or, for a different return route, take the high water access trail. The high water route gradually ascends above Red Creek, following an old railroad grade. At 0.75 mile, the trail abruptly exits the railroad grade to the left, and following a series of steep downhill switchbacks, emerges onto Laneville Road near the bridge over Red Creek.

27

Spruce Knob Recreation Area: Big Run

Distance: 6.9 miles
Time: 4.5 hours
Elevation change: 720 feet
Maps: USGS 7½' Spruce Knob; *Hiking Guide to Monongahela National Forest and Vicinity.*
Highlights: Beaver ponds, Big Run, meadows

The loop hike centered around Big Run makes an ideal day hike during the summer as well as a beautiful cross-country ski outing during the winter. The terrain is very gentle for the majority of the route, and the scenery and wildlife are outstanding. The route along Big Run seems rarely used, providing a refreshing adventure in solitude in surroundings no less beautiful than those of the heavily frequented trails nearby.

The trailhead is on the north side of FS 112 between Spruce Knob Lake and the trailhead for the hike to Spruce Knob (Hike number 30). To reach the trailhead, follow the directions for the Spruce Knob hike, then continue 1.5 miles west of the Spruce Knob trailhead. A grassy pull-off on the north side of the road marks the trailhead. Signs for the trails leaving this point are set back in the woods north of the road. Parking is available in the grassy area.

This point is the southern trailhead for both Big Run of Gandy Trail and Allegheny Mountain Trail. The hike we describe starts along Big Run of Gandy Trail and returns on Allegheny Mountain Trail, but

because this is a loop hike you may take either trail first.

Big Run of Gandy Trail leads downhill to the left of Allegheny Mountain Trail near the edge of the woods north of the parking area beside a sign. Although the descent is steep at first, the path soon descends more gently through trout lilies, ferns, violets, and dwarf ginseng. Blue blazes mark the path as it makes its way through the moist birch and beech forest. After about a quarter of a mile, the trail levels out then fords a pair of small streams. The trail is soggy in spots where it winds along the stream and through small sphagnum-filled seeps.

The trail enters an open meadow along the stream, fording bits and pieces of the stream at about 0.4 mile. From here, the path wanders in and out of the forest edge on the east side of a mile-long stretch of Big Run as it flows through open meadows. Be sure to follow blue blazes. Although the path is slightly graded, it is seldom used, making it difficult to follow in places.

Beaver have created a series of ponds along Big Run starting at about 0.5 mile

Cooling off in Big Run

along the trail. They are working actively in some of the ponds, while other ponds are no longer maintained. The wood duck, one of our most beautiful waterfowl species, has taken up residence in these beaver ponds. The female wood duck returns to her particular beaver pond with great fidelity, nesting in the same nest, or at least nearby, year after year. Her female offspring also will probably nest close by. Marital fidelity, though, is not characteristic of the wood duck breeding system; a female mates with a different male every year, although she is faithful during any one breeding season, a breeding pattern known as serial monogamy. The pair bonding takes place before spring migration in some far off southern wetland where wood ducks from all over congregate for the winter. While the females you see are West Virginia-born and raised, the males could be from Canada, Vermont, or Georgia, because the male is not drawn to his birthplace. Instead, he follows his mate to her native nesting grounds.

After almost 1.5 miles, the path fords Big Run twice in rapid succession. Beyond the second crossing, begin looking for a well-used campsite among a stand of pine trees to the right of the trail. Just beyond these pines, the path crosses a wetland surrounding an incoming creek, which is the North Fork of Big Run. North Fork of Big Run Trail leaves Big Run of Gandy Trail heading northeast immediately before this creek crossing. Although no sign existed at this junction in 1985, the remains of one could be seen scattered in pieces in the meadow. The turn is fairly easy to locate nevertheless. Turn right and follow the blue-blazed trail along the North Fork of Big Run.

The North Fork of Big Run Trail is routed through a beautiful section of forest. The path appears to follow an old railroad or logging road, for it is well-graded. Numerous sites for picnicking and camping can be found along the stream. The path fords all or part of the stream six times before entering an open field where the stream forks. This secluded meadow is an ideal spot to rest and enjoy the stream and surrounding countryside.

North Fork of Big Run Trail leaves the upper north corner of the meadow after fording the right fork of the stream. It continues, slightly ascending along the right fork, to a trail junction at 2.9 miles where a wooden bridge crosses the creek to the left. Here, do not cross the bridge, but instead, continue straight along the grassy trail beside the creek. Signs of beaver activity can be seen soon after the trail junction. Then, at about 2.2 miles, the trail enters a meadow surrounded by a large stand of spruce trees. With a bit of stealth, you can pick your way quietly along the uphill side of this stream-divided meadow and look down on the waterfowl and wildlife as they go about their daily affairs unaware of your presence.

The path gradually changes directions as it skirts along the edge of the meadow so that it leaves the far end of the meadow at about 3.5 miles heading southeast. From here it ascends the mountain through the woods for about 0.4 mile to a ridgetop meadow. The path leaves this meadow on the left side and continues through the woods before entering another meadow with a stand of pines. Just beyond this meadow at 4.5 miles is the intersection with Allegheny Mountain Trail. A sign for Big Run Trail is encountered beside Allegheny Mountain Trail, where you turn right.

Allegheny Mountain Trail is a wide jeep

track that is barred to vehicles. It follows the ridgetop through a forest of beech, maple, and birch. The trail shows signs of vehicle wear, probably by those maintaining wildlife plots along the track. At 5.2 miles, a jeep track intersects from the right. Continue straight along the ridgetop. A meadow can be seen through the trees on the left side of the trail near the end. Just beyond the meadow, you encounter the gate blocking vehicles from the trail. Your car is visible from here, as the trail exits the forest at the parking area.

Dolly Sods Wilderness: Rohrbaugh Plains Trail

Distance: 7.2 miles
Time: 6 hours
Elevation change: 640 feet
Maps: USGS 7½' Hopeville
Highlights: Views, wildflowers, heath barrens

Dolly Sods is one of the most popular wilderness areas in West Virginia. Two of its many attractions are blueberry picking in late summer and viewing the spectacular azalea and laurel blooms in early summer. Native West Virginians are particularly fond of picking the "huckleberries" (blueberries). A family outing for a day of picking at 4,000 feet on Dolly Sods yields gallons of the tiny but tasty fruits. Visitors to the same location earlier in the season will be treated to one of the most delightful natural displays of wildflowers in the entire Appalachians: vast fields of white, light pink, and deep pink azaleas. At the high elevations of Dolly Sods you will come to understand why West Virginia is known as "almost heaven."

The loop hike we describe takes you through a small section of the high-elevation heath barren habitat as well as some typical upland forests. The shortest route to the trail is to turn northwest from WV 28 onto Jordan Run Road ten miles west of Petersburg. You reach a fork in the road at 0.9 mile: from there follow signs to the left to Dolly Sods on FS 19. The road climbs steeply for the next 6.3 miles until you reach an intersection. Our hike includes a section at the end of the

loop along FS 19 and FS 75. To avoid walking along the gravel road, you could set up a shuttle. A vehicle could be stationed at the point where the trail emerges on the road by turning right at this intersection and following FS 75 for 1.4 miles to a pull-off on the left side of the road. The beginning of the hike (with or without a shuttle) is reached by turning left at the intersection and remaining on FS 19 until you reach a picnic area 0.5 mile from the intersection. The parking area is on the left side of the road just north of the picnic area.

Rohrbaugh Plains Trail leaves FS 19 opposite the parking area. The trail is marked with signs at the trailhead and is blue-blazed. You begin the hike in a second-growth forest of yellow birch, cherry, maple and scattered red spruce at an elevation of 4,040 feet. The understory is a mixture of ferns and rhododendron. At 0.9 mile the trail crosses a grassy swath. You cross four small streams in a half-mile. In this section the trail also passes through occasional open meadows, both dry and wet.

Such openings provide important wildlife habitat for game animals such as deer, turkey, and grouse. You may startle a deer in one of these openings, espe-

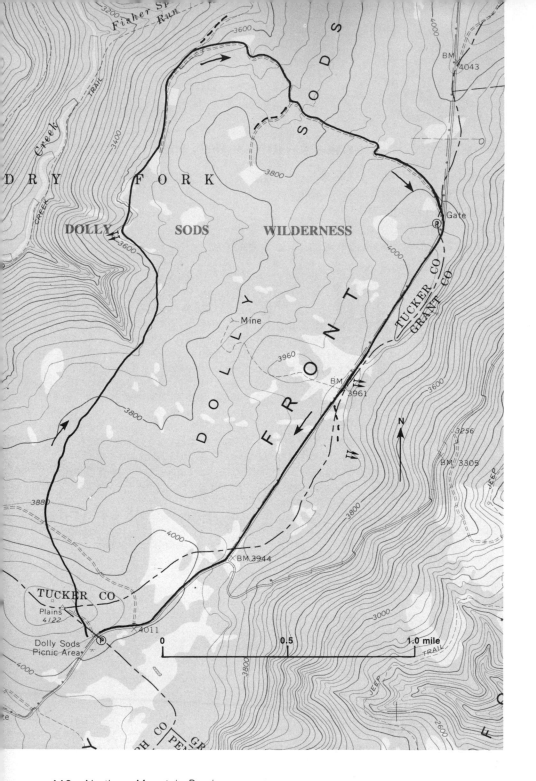

cially early or late in the day. You may be the startled one, though, when you flush a grouse. These heavy birds have one of the loudest takeoffs in the avian world, and they always seem to wait until you are about to step on them before whooshing up and out of your way.

The trail follows a railroad grade beginning at 2.4 miles, and you cross more small streams three times in the next half-mile or so. All these streams eventually flow into Red Creek about 1,000 vertical feet below you to the northwest. At 3.1 miles you cross a major tributary stream about seven feet across. Soon after this crossing, the trail nears the edge of the steep drop into the valley of Red Creek. A short spur trail to the left leads to a rock outcrop with a spectacular view a few yards off the trail. From here you can look down into the valley and across to Breathed Mountain on the opposite side.

The trail continues north and reaches a clearing with campsites at 3.4 miles. Another clearing follows at 3.6 miles. To continue the loop hike, watch for a right turn off Rohrbaugh Plains Trail onto a wildlife trail just before reaching this second clearing near a small stream. There are blue blazes near the stream and a double blue blaze just prior to the turn.

The wildlife trail enters an open field with rock cairns marking the path. At the far end of the clearing the trail joins an old railroad grade. A small road makes a right fork at 4.0 miles, while the trail continues along the railroad grade to the left.

At 4.6 miles you enter a meadow, skirting the right edge, and then leave the meadow to the right. A side trail to a maintained wildlife clearing turns right at 5.2 miles and you continue straight ahead, intersecting with FS 75 at 5.3 miles. If you have set up a shuttle, your car is in the parking lot near the end of the wildlife trail. To hike the full circuit,

Pink azalea

turn right on FS 75, and follow the road back to the picnic area.

Along the road you may encounter some interesting and showy plants such as wild bleeding-heart and fireweed. Fireweed is a tall, herbaceous perennial with pink flowers arranged in a spike around one main stem. This species is cosmopolitan, being found in disturbed areas from the arctic south to Georgia in the mountains. Its name comes from its abundance as an early successional species following fire, but here on Dolly Sods, and elsewhere high in the Appalachians, it also becomes established along roadsides.

In places along the road you will also encounter small patches of vegetation dominated by heath plants, plants in the *Ericaceae* family. The best examples of heath barrens may be seen farther to the north on FS 75 near Red Creek Campground and Bear Rocks. Even in the small communities seen on this hike, you can find up to eight or nine plant species from this family living side by side. These plants include rhododendron, mountain laurel, azalea, two or three species of blueberry, huckleberry, trailing arbutus, and teaberry.

A few miles from Dolly Sods two very unusual heath plants were discovered: cross-leaf heath and heather. These two plants must have been introduced artifi-

cially, for their native home is in the British Isles. Perhaps some homesick immigrant from Scotland or Ireland planted them to remind him of the fatherland. At any rate, the populations have slowly spread and seem to have made themselves right at home with their West Virginia heath relatives.

On the east side of FS 75 at 6.1 miles a rock outcrop affords superb views toward Seneca Rocks and North Fork Mountain. Another overlook with a pullout for visitors is reached at 6.3 miles. A spur trail leads southeast away from the road to the overlook. Nearby you may observe areas where the rocks seem to have been heaved out of the ground in a distinct pattern. Some geologists believe this is evidence of the type of rock sorting that accompanies permafrost (frozen soil) activity today in arctic climates. There is no permafrost at Dolly Sods today, but we can speculate that at the height of the last glaciation this area might have been much like arctic tundra. If temperatures were cold enough, the soils could have remained frozen year-round. The freeze-thaw action of surface layers with the changing seasons would have produced the rock sorting patterns seen here.

FS 75 meets FS 19 at 6.7 miles, and you go straight to your car at the picnic ground.

Laurel River Trail

Distance: 8.0 miles
Time: 6 hours
Elevation change: 80 feet
Maps: USGS 7½′ Sinks of Gandy
Highlights: Glades, beaver activity

*We need the tonic of wilderness, to wade
sometimes in marshes where the bittern
and the meadow-hen lurk, and hear the
booming of the snipe: to smell the whisper-
ing sedge where only some wilder and
more solitary fowl builds her nest, and the
mink crawls with its belly close to the
ground.*

Henry David Thoreau, Walden

The headwaters of Laurel Fork River run
through some of the most remote National Forest lands in West Virginia. Signs of
man and his past activities abound, yet
the solitude and wildness of the area
give you the feeling of a land returning to
wilderness. Laurel River Trail is an ideal
day hike for those needing the tonic of a
quiet outing, far from crowds of tourists
and sightseers. It would also make a nice
cross-country ski trip for advanced skiers.
The only limiting element on this hike is
that the trail crosses Laurel Fork twice
without a bridge. In times of high water
the route may be impassable.

Here we describe the southern section
of Laurel River Trail between a trailhead
on Forest Service road 14 and Laurel
Fork Campground. The hike is best done
with a shuttle, although day hikes from
either end are possible.

To reach the northern terminus of the
hike, turn south from US 33 at Wymer
opposite an Ashland gas station onto FS
14 (Middle Mountain Road). Five miles
south of that turn you pass a trailhead of
the northern section of Laurel River Trail
(not described here). Twelve miles south
of US 33 you reach an intersection
where you continue south (straight
ahead) toward Thornwood. Just 0.25 mile
past this intersection you come to a fork
in the road. Turn left at the fork onto
County Route 40, and drive 1.5 miles to
reach Laurel Fork Campground and the
northern end of the hike. The campground is in a large, open field on the
right side of the road. Parking is available
on the edge of this field by the entrance
to the campground.

The southern beginning of the hike is
reached by continuing south on FS 14
(straight ahead) at the fork in the road
where CR 40 leaves FS 14. The trailhead, and a small space to park, is
found 8.1 miles from the fork on the left
(east) side of FS 14.

Laurel River Trail (#306 on national
forest maps) starts out on a gated forest
service road (FS 97). A sign at the trailhead indicates that nearby forest plots
have been set aside for silvicultural (tree
growth) experiments. The rocky road

leads through a beautiful forest of tall, straight black cherry and maple. One mile from the trailhead, watch for a brown post (a former trail sign) on the side of the road, and a small, grassy clearing on the left. Note also a tree marked with blue blazes at the clearing. Laurel River Trail, marked intermittently with blue blazes, turns left at this point.

The trail gradually descends to a tributary of Laurel Fork at 1.6 miles. The next half-mile is through an open glade on either side of the tributary, dotted with planted Norway Spruce. Carpets of club-mosses flank the trail.

At 2.0 miles, the trail crosses over the tributary and soon meets a larger, more shrubby glade. The tributary stream joins Laurel Fork in this glade, and the trail bends left, following the edge of the glade. Excellent bird watching can be expected along the forest edge in spring. At 2.4 miles the trail meets Laurel Fork, following its left bank downstream. The trail becomes obscure at this point, and blazes may be difficult to locate.

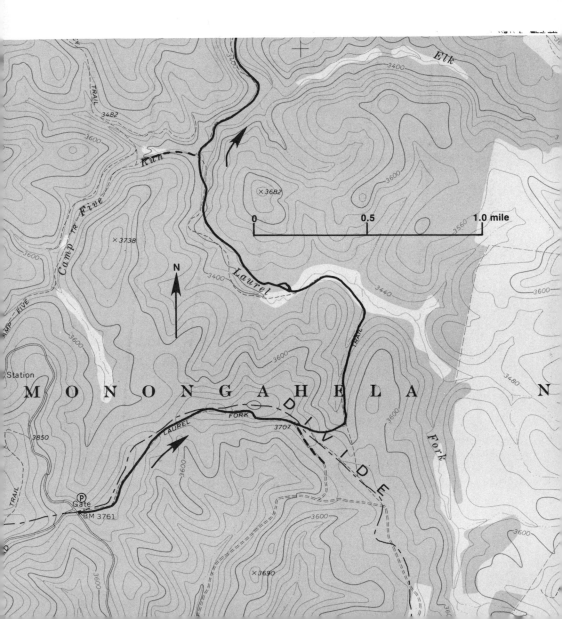

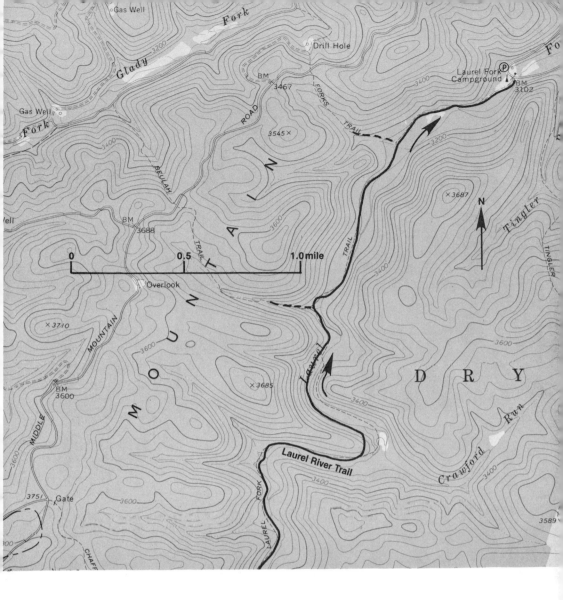

If you lose the trail hopelessly, don't panic. Bushwhack downstream and you will eventually meet up with Laurel River Trail again. The key to finding the trail here is to look for a pine forest set back from the river on the opposite bank. If you look carefully, you may be able to see blue blazes on trees at the edge of the pine woods. If you come to a large steep bank on the near side of the river,

you have gone too far. Near an old beaver dam and house, you cross the river and walk through a meadow toward the pine forest. The river can be quite deep in spots, so choose your crossing well—the top of an old beaver dam is a good place if you can find one intact.

As you approach the pines, the path and blue blazes should become more obvious. At 2.7 and 2.8 miles you come

A grass inflorescence in a meadow
near Laurel Fork

to potential tent sites within the stand of pines. A second confusing place in the trail is reached as you leave the pine forest. The trail splits here, with both branches bending to the right. One fork climbs uphill, and the other traverses the slope above the river. They soon come together again. Avoid continuing straight ahead into the low marshy area by the river.

At 3.3 miles the trail comes to another clearing near the stream. Blue blazes on a hemlock tree at the far side of the clearing mark the path. The trail crosses the river again beyond the hemlock. This crossing is easier than the first.

Camp Five Trail (#315), also blue-blazed, joins Laurel River Trail from the left at 3.6 miles. Forty yards beyond this junction, Laurel River Trail crosses a small creek and follows it toward Laurel Fork. The trail passes to the left of a virgin stand of red spruce at 4.1 miles.

Beaver activity is evident along much of Laurel Fork. Before widespread trapping began in the early 1700s, many of the small drainages in West Virginia supported large beaver populations. By 1825, the beaver were nearly gone throughout what is now West Virginia. In the 1930s, though, sixty-four beavers were introduced for restocking, and today, beavers are making a dramatic comeback, especially in remote areas such as Laurel Fork.

The return of this fine animal is clearly a vital step in restoring the area to wilderness. The beaver, a native of our wilderness, is important in providing habitat for numerous other species. Ducks such as the mallard, black, and wood duck will nest and raise young near beaver ponds. Shallow-water feeders such as herons and American bitterns are drawn to pond edges. Muskrats, mink, frogs, salamanders, and crayfish all benefit from the activities of beaver. Even when an old beaver pond drains, the area often will become a grassy meadow that supports important wildlife species such as deer, grouse, turkey, and numerous songbirds. Indirectly, the beaver influences a wide array of species that, taken as a group, add tremendous diversity and authenticity to our wilderness experiences.

At 4.4 miles the trail passes under a rock outcrop next to the stream. A nice campsite is found here. Another campsite is found at 4.9 miles in a flat area below the trail. The trail passes through a pretty birch forest at 5.5 miles.

Beulah Trail, another access to Laurel Fork from FS 14, joins Laurel River Trail from the left at 6.4 miles. At 7.3 miles, just beyond a clearing, Forks Trail comes in from the left. This is another access trail from FS 14. At 7.8 miles the trail reaches Laurel Fork Campground. County Route 40 (and your car) is 0.2 mile away at the far end of the campground.

Spruce Knob Recreation Area: Spruce Knob

Distance: Seneca Creek-Lumberjack Trail Loop 8.1 miles;
  Seneca Creek-Spruce Knob Shuttle 8.7 miles
Time: 5-6 hours
Elevation change: Loop 760 feet; Shuttle 1,600 feet
Maps: USGS 7½' Whitmer, Spruce Knob; *Hiking Guide to
  Monongahela National Forest and Vicinity*
Highlights: Views, Judy Springs, sinks

Seneca Creek has its origins among the spruces and black cherries on the northwest flank of Spruce Mountain. A small trickle of icy clear water quickly grows to a stream of sparkling waterfalls and wild beauty as it drops to join the North Fork of the South Branch of the Potomac River. Rising above the banks of Seneca Creek is the highest point in West Virginia, Spruce Knob, with an elevation of 4,861 feet.

Spruce Knob is actually a misnomer, for the summit does not form a distinct knob. The highest point is only slightly higher than the rest of the long flat-topped ridge of Spruce Mountain. The summit is wild, windswept, and often enshrouded in fog. On a clear day, the view can be spectacular, but in the fog the mood becomes eerie and almost mystical.

The trail system we describe is in the Spruce Knob–Seneca Rocks National Recreation Area of the Monongahela National Forest. Access is easiest from US 33 between Riverton and Judy Gap. Take Briery Gap Run Road west from US 33 1.5 miles south of Riverton, or 0.5 mile north of Judy Gap. Follow the signs to Spruce Knob for 10.2 miles. At this point, the Forest Service road forks.

Spruce Knob is to the right 1.8 miles, and the trailhead we describe, Seneca Creek Trail, is to the left approximately four miles down Forest Service Road 112.

There are three hiking options. The first option is a loop beginning on Seneca Creek Trail and ending with Lumberjack Trail. The second is from Seneca Creek Trail to Spruce Knob observation tower on Huckleberry Trail. The latter option involves returning via the Forest Service road to the trailhead, or setting up a shuttle between the mountaintop and the trailhead . Another possibility would be to make an overnight backpacking trip out of the Spruce Knob climb. Judy Springs Campground could serve as base camp, and Spruce Knob would then be a 10.6 mile round trip from Judy Springs.

Parking at Seneca Creek trailhead is available in a lot on the north side of Forest Service Road 112. The trailhead begins on an old dirt road blocked to vehicle traffic. On the left of the trail is a stand of young cherry and red spruce, to the right is a red spruce plantation. The trail gradually descends, passing meadows dotted with spruce, hawthorn,

Spider webs in the early morning sun

and black cherry. This portion of the trail was a railroad bed during the logging era.

Logging played a major role in this area in the early 1900s. Dr. Roy Clarkson, a West Virginia botanist, has written a fascinating account of the logging history of this area in his book, *Tumult in the Mountains*. Red spruce was the most valuable timber tree. Tall red spruce of sixty to ninety feet were common, and some trees grew to diameters of six feet

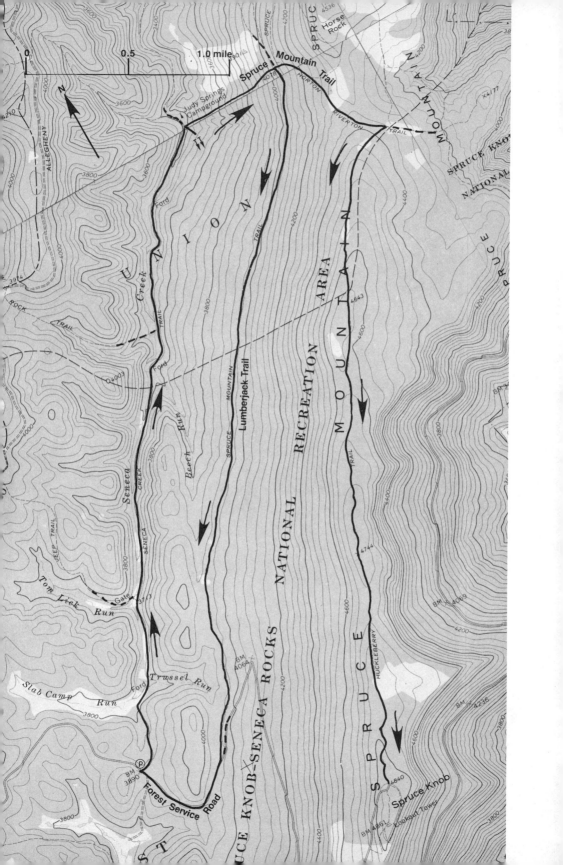

or more, yielding five sixteen-foot logs. Imagine hiking in such a forest with a thick and impenetrable understory of rhododendron. Tales are told of hunters venturing too far into these forests and becoming lost or entangled in the rhododendron thickets, never to be seen again.

The path crosses a small stream coming down from the right. Signs of past beaver activity become evident within the first 0.25 mile. Tom Lick Run Trail departs to the left at 1.0 mile through an area seeded to game food. Seneca Creek is by now about five feet wide, having grown from a small trickle at the trailhead. Two miles down Seneca Creek Trail, the path crosses another tributary coming from the right. The next intersection at 2.4 miles is with Swallow Rock Trail, which forks to the left.

Continue along Seneca Creek Trail to Judy Springs Campground straight ahead. The path to Judy Springs is very level. It is ideal for cross-country skiing when Forest Service Road 112 is passable. (This road is not maintained in winter, so four-wheel drive may be required to gain access to the trail system through snow.)

Seneca Creek continues to grow in size as you hike down the trail. It flows through beautiful open woodlands between birch-lined banks, making an enchanting scene. Near Judy Springs Campground, the path crosses a bridge to the opposite bank of Seneca Creek where the waterfalls of Judy Springs cascade over rock ledges.

Judy Springs Campground is located 3.4 miles from the trailhead. The site is a primitive walk-in campground situated in a lovely pastoral setting. Tent sites, a water pump, and a latrine are available. A sign at the pump points to Judy Springs Trail and Spruce Knob Trail to the right. Bear Hunter Trail and Horton-Horserock Trail are straight ahead.

Take the right fork across Seneca Creek to Judy Springs. Once across the footbridge, the path forks again. The right-most fork leads to Judy Springs, while the middle fork leads to Spruce Knob. The left fork passes some tent sites along the bank of Seneca Creek. The right fork to Judy Springs winds up the hill among small birches and across a small stream coming down a steep embankment. Upon closer viewing, you will see the stream flows straight out of the mountainside. Just beyond the crest of the next knoll, an even larger stream erupts from the mountain forming a small waterfall. These are Judy Springs.

After viewing Judy Springs, retrace your steps to the middle fork to follow Spruce Knob Trail. The trail begins with a gentle ascent and is blazed in blue. Within a short distance, the trail breaks into a beautiful open meadow on the mountainside. The trail crosses a broken-down stile or gate, then climbs the meadow diagonally to the woods near the opposite corner. Rock cairns and wooden stakes mark the path. From the meadow, the view of Seneca Creek Valley and the ridge beyond is unblemished.

At the top of the meadow a sign pointing to the right reads "Spruce Knob, 5 miles." The trail skirts the edge of the forest above the meadow from north to south, then leaves the meadow across another dilapidated stile or gate. Just beyond is the trail intersection where Lumberjack Trail leaves Spruce Knob Trail.

Lumberjack Trail

For a loop hike, take Lumberjack Trail to the right. This trail follows along an old railroad bed. The path is often wet, as it crosses a small stream and many seepages where small springs bubble from the mountainside. The trail takes you through a picturesque forest of maple, yellow birch, and beech. The highlight of this trail is a pair of sinks. Sinks are places where streams disappear into the ground (springs in reverse).

Just beyond an old meadow to the west of the trail about 2.9 miles from the Spruce Knob Trail intersection is a depressed area with steep slopes near a grove of hemlocks. In wet weather, this is an active sink. The streambed usually is swept clean of debris by the stream. Just a little farther down the trail, a sizable stream winds its way through the forest to disappear with an audible splash into a dark crack in the forest floor. There are several ice caves in the cliffside where ice formed in the winter in the deep crevices stays frozen until late in the summer. Cool air wafts across your face if you peer into the damp blackness between the rocks.

The Lumberjack Trail intersects Forest Road 112 a little over 0.6 mile beyond the sinks. At this intersection, turn right and follow the road 0.6 mile to the parking lot and your vehicle.

Spruce Knob Trail

If Spruce Knob is your destination, you will continue on Spruce Knob Trail at the intersection with Lumberjack Trail. Shortly after leaving Lumberjack Trail, the path comes to a small clearing and in 400 yards to a larger clearing spotted with spruce trees. These meadows are only a hint of what is to come. The similarity of the country to open tundra will become stronger as you ascend the mountain. These lower meadows are a mixture of grasses, ferns, blueberries, and goldenrod. About 0.6 mile beyond the Lumberjack Trail intersection you reach a junction with Huckleberry Trail. Turn right onto Huckleberry Trail toward Spruce Knob.

As you ascend, the clearings, with their mixture of heath plants such as huckleberries and laurel, become more prevalent. Rock cairns serve as trail guides through the heath meadows as the trail meanders through fireweed, alder patches, wild bleeding-heart, dwarf dogwood, and lady's-slipper. Near the top of the mountain, remnants of an old airplane wreck may be found along the trail. The views become spectacular both to the right into Seneca Creek Valley and beyond and to the left toward Shenandoah Mountain.

The trail is rocky at the top. Stripes of lichen-encrusted boulders, gathered and sorted by frost action, divide the patches of heath and spruce. The spruce trees are stunted and windshaped, with most of their branches near the ground, below heights susceptible to winter snow blast, or on the lee side of the tree. The path ends in the parking lot of the observation tower 4.7 miles from the intersection with Lumberjack Trail.

Fire has been very important in molding the vegetation on Spruce Knob. According to Dr. Earl Core, a well-known West Virginia botanist, the top of Spruce Knob was formerly a dense forest of spruce and birch. Some areas were burned purposely to clear pasture lands, while other areas were destroyed by fires from careless settlers. Then lumber companies built railroads to the top of the mountain and denuded large areas. Fires, probably started by sparks from the trains, again ravaged the area. A Marlinton resident has been quoted as saying Spruce Knob was known locally as "The Big Burn."

Since the Forest Service began management of the area in 1921, the vegetation has changed only slowly. The most conspicuous change is the increase in the number and size of the red spruce trees. Still, these wind-blasted trees are a far cry from the extensive forests of spruce and birch that originally covered West Virginia's loftiest summit.

31

Otter Creek Wilderness Area

Distance: 15.7 miles
Time: 1 to 3 days
Elevation change: 2,432 feet
Maps: USGS 7½′ Mozark Mountain, Parsons, Bowden,
   Harman
Highlights: Waterfalls, pools, wilderness, overnight shelters

Large, unbroken tracts of wilderness are uncommon in West Virginia. Cranberry Backcountry and Dolly Sods are probably the best-known of such areas in the state. Less well-known, but easily on a par with those two in terms of quality, is Otter Creek Wilderness near Parsons. The centerpiece of the wilderness is Otter Creek itself. Otter Creek is a picture book stream: not so large as to be impractical to cross on foot (except at flood stage), yet not so small that you can't take a refreshing swim on a hot summer day. The stream cascades over numerous waterfalls in its rapid descent, resting only momentarily in deep, crystal-clear pools below each fall. Ridges on either side of Otter Creek tower a thousand feet above the valley floor. Two Adirondack-style lean-tos provide shelter for overnight backpacking.

The hike we describe takes you to the high ridges of Green Mountain and Shavers Mountain, as well as along the most beautiful stretch of Otter Creek. The trip is best done in two or perhaps three days for maximum enjoyment, although hikers who are in excellent shape could complete the circuit in one long day.

To reach the trailhead, drive to Parsons, and turn east on US 219. Still in Parsons, turn south off US 219 opposite the "Big Tee" restaurant onto a street marked with a sign for Otter Creek Wilderness. A few yards past the turnoff you cross a railroad track and immediately turn left on the next street (not marked with a sign). At the first bend in the road you will see another sign pointing to wilderness trailheads.

The trail we describe begins at Big Springs Gap (5.7 miles from the sign). The paved road becomes gravel-surfaced near a cemetery 0.8 mile beyond the sign. You take the left fork in the road at 1.3 miles. A mile beyond this fork (2.3 miles) you bear right on Forest Service road 701 at an unmarked fork in the road, going uphill away from Dry Fork River. You enter Fernow Experimental Forest, a research area for the Forest Service, at 2.5 miles. A sign explaining the uses of the Experimental Forest is reached at 3.2 miles. Stay on the main road (FS 701), ignoring side roads, until you come to another fork at 5.1 miles. Turn left at this fork and you will reach the Big Springs Gap trailhead and a small pullout on the left side of the road (5.7 miles).

A trail register is provided near the pull-off. At the outset, Big Springs Gap

trail (#154) is rocky and well-worn, as it is one of the major access trails to the roadless wilderness area. The trail quickly descends to Spring Run from Big Springs Gap, then follows this seasonal stream 420 vertical feet to Otter Creek. At 0.8 mile you will notice evidence of heavy winds as the trail passes a patch of forest with many down or broken trees. The understory here has responded to the gap with verdant growth. The full descent is covered in 0.9 mile when the trail reaches Otter Creek. Several obvious campsites may be found here.

The trail crosses Otter Creek here. Signs warn of the danger of flash flooding during heavy rains. On the east side of Otter Creek, Big Springs Gap Trail meets Otter Creek Trail (#131). Signs at this junction give distances to numerous possible destinations. You turn right (south) at the junction on Otter Creek.

Otter Creek Trail is wide and scenic here, sandwiched between Otter Creek and a fifteen-foot high cliff. The cliff is covered with ferns, mosses, and wildflowers. One particularly interesting fern is the walking fern. You may not recognize the plant as a fern at first. It has small one- to ten- inch arrow-shaped fronds with straight margins. You will find it in damp spots along the cliffside, especially on sloping soil where leaf litter cannot accumulate because of the angle of the slope. As with other small plants such as mosses and lichens, being small means that accumulation of litter—especially litter of large, deciduous leaves—would cause intense shading, resulting in death.

The name walking fern comes from its unusual method of vegetative spread. The fronds of this tiny fern expand continuously, eventually reaching three to ten inches in length. The frond tip then sags to touch the soil. Where the tip meets the soil a new plant is formed. The cycle repeats itself, and if you could map the position of the fern you would see that, over time, the plant actually does "walk."

about in the available habitat.

At 1.4 miles the trail bends away from the river slightly. The forest is dominated by hemlock, birch, maple, and tulip poplar near the stream. At 1.9 miles, more evidence of wind damage to the forest is visible.

Otter Creek Trail meets Green Mountain Trail at 2.0 miles. Clearly written trail signs again give mileages to various destinations. The route we describe goes left here on Green Mountain Trail, eventually returning to this junction from the south via Otter Creek Trail.

Green Mountain Trail, marked with blue blazes, turns east away from the creek. Within 0.1 mile, a campsite is found on the right side of the trail. Soon after, the trail begins a steady ascent of the flanks of Green Mountain. At 2.2 miles the path crosses a small intermittent stream.

While you are hiking this circuit trail, you may want to watch for signs of black bear—paw prints in the mud, or perhaps badly clawed trees or trail signs. These normally shy animals are common in the wilderness, although they are seen by very few hikers. Nevertheless, you may wish to take precautionary measures with your food at night if you are backpacking, for example, by hanging it from a high tree limb. Bears are omnivorous, and are known to eat freeze-dried food and granola quite contentedly.

If you do encounter a bear, day or night, be very cautious and respectful, but do not panic or run. If you do, the bear might treat you as a prey animal trying to escape. This is exactly what you don't want to be because you could not possibly outrun or outfight a black bear. This warning is aptly phrased in a famous short poem:

> Man, bear,
> Struggling pair,
> Man, inferior,
> Gone interior!

As common sense would tell you, don't try to physically or verbally scare off the bear either. Most likely the bear will leave the scene, as any shy animal would, once it realizes that a human is nearby. The most dangerous situation occurs when a bear (or worse, a bear's cub) feels threatened, for example, if it is cornered, or if it is guarding a food item. Again rapid flight is not a good idea, but a measured retreat would definitely be in order.

After you have lived or hiked in bear country a while, fear eventually turns into healthy respect. You no longer look over your shoulder with every step. You know that a bear encounter is unlikely because of the natural shyness of the animals. You also know that if an encounter occurs, the chances are very small, if you are respectful, that the encounter will be a bad one. The attitude of respect you take with you in bear territory becomes part of the wilderness experience, a part that is humbling, and good for humans, who invariably think of themselves as apart from, and not part of, the natural web of living things.

As Green Mountain Trail ascends, the understory species typical of dry sites become more common. A thick patch of greenbrier prevents you from wandering off the path. The trail finally begins to level out at an elevation of 3,300 feet as it approaches the top of Green Mountain.

At 3.5 miles the trail bends sharply left and thereafter follows an old railroad grade. The path crosses a flat, wet area and a small stream at 3.7 miles. After continuing straight across the relatively flat ridgetop, the trail bends right at 4.1 miles, leaving the railroad grade and following a muddy track through a beech and hemlock forest. The trail rejoins the railroad grade at 4.4 miles and crosses another stream at 4.6 miles. This stream may be the last reliable water until you reach more streams on Mylius Trail, four miles ahead.

Just beyond the stream is a small clearing with a campsite. Possession Camp Trail joins Green Mountain Trail here. Stay to the left on Green Mountain Trail. The trail is occasionally difficult to follow past this point, so watch carefully for blue blazes.

At 5.1 miles the trail reaches a high point on the ridge with a stand of spruce on the left side of the trail. The trail comes to a small clearing with a campsite at 5.5 miles and meets Shavers Mountain Trail (#129) at 5.9 miles. Shavers Mountain Trail has been abandoned north of this point, so you can only turn right at this junction following arrows toward the shelter. The trail is not blazed.

Another intersection is reached at 6.4 miles where a spur trail to one of the trail shelters leaves Shavers Mountain Trail. Even if you are not staying overnight there, the short (0.15 mile) side trip is worth your effort. The shelter sits in a small clearing on the edge of the steep east face of Shavers Mountain at an elevation of 3,700 feet. The view to the east toward Middle Mountain and Rich Mountain is superb. In the distance you can also see the high peaks of Mount Porte Crayon to the north (elevation 4,769 feet) and Spruce Knob, West Virginia's highest peak (4,861 feet) to the south.

Retrace your steps to Shavers Mountain Trail and turn left (south). At 6.9 miles the trail enters a virgin forest of spruce and hemlock. A particularly large (three-foot diameter) hemlock is reached at 7.2 miles. The trees are a mixture of sizes and ages in contrast to most forests in West Virginia. When the trail leaves the uncut woods at 7.5 miles, the contrast is immediately evident.

Trail shelter on Shavers Mountain

The trail passes through a small clearing at 7.9 miles, then drops down on the east side of the ridgetop at 8.3 miles. Mylius Trail (#128) intersects from the right at 8.8 miles, and a campsite may be found near this junction. Signs again indicate distances to various destinations. You turn right on Mylius Trail toward Otter Creek.

The trail begins an immediate descent to the west toward Otter Creek. You pass a couple of clearings on the way down (9.0 miles). Soon you can hear the rushing water of Otter Creek. At 9.6 miles Mylius Trail reaches and crosses Otter Creek, meeting Otter Creek Trail on the far side.

At the trail junction a pair of trail signs orient you once again with respect to possible destinations. From here the trail follows Otter Creek in its precipitous journey downstream. There are many campsites near the trail in this stretch. When the trail is not adjacent to the stream, small spur trails lead to overlooks for views of the many waterfalls and pools.

At 10.2 miles the trail recrosses the stream. A junction with Possession Camp Trail is reached at 10.7 miles. Near this junction is a particularly large swimming hole and just downstream from here is the second lean-to. Several campsites are also located near the shelter. At the end of the clearing where the trail shelter sits, the trail crosses the creek again (10.8 miles). A series of beautiful cascades follow. At 13.5 miles you recross the creek and reach the junction with Green Mountain Trail at 13.7 miles.

Continue downstream on Otter Creek Trail to the intersection with Big Springs Gap Trail (14.8 miles). Turn left and climb the last 0.9 mile to the trailhead and your vehicle.

Southern Mountain Province

32

Cranberry Glades

Distance: 1/2 mile
Time: 1/2 hour
Elevation change: None
Maps: USGS 7½' Lobelia; Visitors' Center pamphlet
Highlights: Northern plant and animal species

Cranberry Glades Botanical Area is one of the more popular natural attractions of West Virginia. Many of the birds, mammals, and plants in the 750-acre tract are more characteristic of regions farther north. Hikers without a keen botanical interest may find the hike itself disappointing. The glades are simply open areas surrounded by extensive alder thickets and bog forest. To anyone who is a botanist at heart, though, the glades are extremely intriguing.

Cranberry Glades is in the southwestern part of Pocahontas County, West Virginia, just twenty miles west of the Virginia state line. The area may be reached from WV 39/ WV 150 east of Richwood. The spur road north off WV 39/150 to the Glades parking lot is well-marked. The parking lot is 1.5 miles from this turnoff on the right side of the spur road. A sign guides visitors to the trailhead.

Open bogs or peatlands, locally known as glades, are common in the mountains of West Virginia. Cranberry Glades are the largest. The "level" bog area is about three miles long and one mile wide in places. Even though the area appears

Boardwalk through Round Glade

level, it drops about forty-five feet in the three miles. The peat covering the bog floor varies in thickness from place to place, with the thickest formation over eleven feet. Analysis of peat collected from the deepest layers shows that the bottom layer of peat is about 9,500 years old.

Mountains surrounding the Glades rise to heights of 4,000 to 4,600 feet, while the bog floor is between 3,350 and 3,400 feet in elevation. This bowl-like setting makes for the severe climate of the bog. Temperatures here frequently are the lowest in the state, as the cold air drains from the surrounding mountains.

In the past 10,000 years, cold-adapted species have migrated northward because of the warming climate and melting of the Pleistocene ice sheets. Because it offers a small zone of cool climate, Cranberry Glades is a refuge for species of plants and animals now more common farther north. Birds that are found at their southernmost known breeding habitats in Eastern North America at the Glades include the hermit thrush, the olive-backed thrush, the mourning warbler, the northern water-thrush and the purple finch.

A number of plants approach their

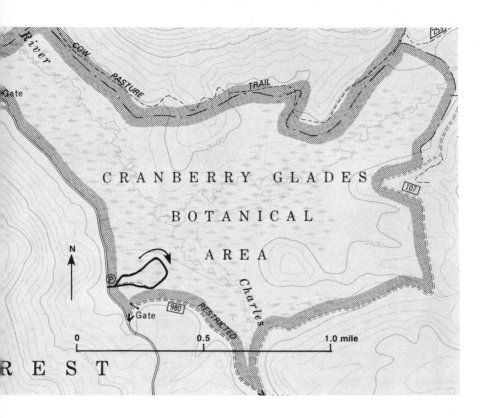

southernmost limit in the Glades, including dwarf dogwood (*Cornus canadensis*), goldthread (*Coptis groenlandica*), buckbean (*Menyanthes trifoliata*), bog rosemary (*Andromeda glaucophylla*) and oak fern (*Dryopteris disjuncta*). Cranberries (*Vaccinium oxycoccos, Vaccinium macrocarpon*) grow in abundance in the open glades and have served as a source of income for some of the local people.

Carnivorous plants, which supplement their mineral requirements by trapping and digesting insects, are also found in the Glades. These include sundew (*Drosera rotundifolia*) and horned bladderwort (*Utricularia cornuta*), which both are native to West Virginia. Pitcher plant (*Sarracenia purpurea*), a carnivorous plant that is not native to West Virginia, is also found in the Glades along the boardwalk. On July 10, 1946, H. P. Sturm planted a specimen that is still flourishing.

Three plant communities are found in the glades. These are the shrub community, the bog forest community, and the open glades community. Each community is distinct in appearance and plant species composition. The shrub community forms a broad belt along the streams and open glades. In this community, alders grow so thick and twisted that whole botany classes plus their professors have been lost for hours trying to find their way back to their cars!

The bog forest community is usually on the edge of the boggy area. Trees such as red spruce and hemlock are the dominant species in this community. Yellow birch and black ash are also found interspersed. Beneath the trees grow shrubs such as winterberry, wild raisin, rhododendron, and yew. Beneath them is a mat of sphagnum moss and wood sorrel with other scattered wildflowers.

The open glades community resembles the treeless arctic tundra in aspect. Mosses and sedges form the bog floor while lichens, cranberries, orchids, and many other wildflowers grow among the sphagnum and sedges. The open glades usually are spongy with water. The community is extremely fragile, and a boardwalk has been built to preserve it yet let people enjoy it.

To reach the boardwalk, take the paved trail leading through the bog forest of giant hemlocks and rhododendron. When you reach the boardwalk and the large welcome sign, take the left fork of the boardwalk loop. The trail leads first through Round Glade, then through Flag Glade. The three plant communities are very distinct here. As you start down the boardwalk, you are walking through the bog forest community. As the path emerges into the open before Round Glade, you hike through a thin band of the shorter shrub community, which surrounds the entire open bog area. The boardwalk then emerges into the eight-acre open bog area of Round Glade.

Cranberries usually are abundant in different stages of development on the carpet of sphagnum. Somewhat shriveled berries formed in the previous year may even be present. These are especially tasty, for often they are slightly fermented. The boardwalk takes you along the edge of the open glade area next to the band of alders. At the opposite end of Round Glade, the trail bends right into the bog forest to emerge in twenty-eight-acre Flag Glade. Sundews and pitcher plants grow right along the boardwalk in Flag Glade. These carnivorous plants are so small and inconspicuous it is easy to overlook them. One group of them grows right beside the interpretive sign describing them.

After going through Flag Glade, the trail reenters the bog forest. The boardwalk crosses Yew Creek several times and returns to the starting point with the welcome sign. At the intersection, turn left and retrace the path to the parking lot.

Just before the end of the boardwalk you will see a wonderful example of a nurse log, on top of which is growing a colony of well-established trees. The bog floor is often too wet for seedling trees to start. When a tree falls and begins to decay, however, it forms a high, relatively dry place that is a perfect site for seeds of hemlocks and other species to get started. This is just what happened here. The fallen tree in decay left only a long thin mound where several hemlocks have germinated and grown to maturity. The roots of these trees grew around the dead log to the bog floor. The decay and sinking of the log left the tops of the roots standing bare, so these trees look as if they are standing in line on their tiptoes.

33

Falls of Hills Creek

Distance: 1 mile
Time: 1 hour
Elevation change: 240 feet
Maps: USGS 7½′ Lobelia
Highlights: Three sets of waterfalls

This short and scenic hike takes you past three waterfalls, one of which rivals Blackwater Falls as the highest waterfall in West Virginia. Upper Falls drops twenty feet, Middle Falls drops forty-five feet, and Lower Falls plunges a full sixty-three feet in a clear drop to a shallow pool below. Between Upper Falls and Lower Falls, Hills Creek drops 220 feet.

Falls of Hills Creek is located approximately five miles west of Cranberry Glades Botanical Area on WV 39. The entrance on the south side of WV 39 is well-marked by a sign. A short road leads to a parking lot at the trailhead.

The trail begins as a gravel path descending to the left of a sign on the edge of the woods at the south end of the parking lot. A short distance into the woods, Forked Mountain Trail leaves to the right of the path beside a sign. Follow the left fork at this intersection to the overlook at Upper Falls. From the overlook you can peer over the brink of Upper Falls as it clears the ledge. Hills Creek sparkles as it flows through the woodland below the falls.

Continue from the overlook along the trail to Middle Falls. The path makes a short ascent to rejoin Forked Mountain Trail. Turn left at this intersection and

descend the moderate slope of the mountainside above Hills Creek. The trail is a wooden boardwalk with guardrails until it reaches the level of Hills Creek. After leading across a bridge over the creek, the trail forks. Take the right fork to Middle Falls overlook; the left Fork goes to Lower Falls.

To gain a different perspective on Middle Falls, return to the last intersection and follow the path to Lower Falls. Beyond the spur to Middle Falls overlook, the trail was not maintained in 1985. The path makes a sharp right and skirts beneath a cliff face. The wooden stairs that originally formed the path in this section are rotting away, so care must be taken to avoid the rotten sections. In some places, this requires scrambling down the mountainside beside the stairs. The path, though, leads to a wonderful view of Middle Falls from below. From this vantage point you can also look downstream and see where the water plunges over the ledge forming Lower Falls.

It is no easy feat to get to Lower Falls. At one time the path was maintained, and we hope it soon will be again. A tree

Lower Falls

FALLS OF
HILLS CREEK
SCENIC AREA

N

0.5 mile

Falls

has fallen across the path as it makes the final descent to the base of Lower Falls. This part of the hike requires using your hands and feet to negotiate the steep section across the main trunk and branches of the downed tree. Just beyond the downed tree, the trail makes a switchback leading under another cliff, and then finally ends at 0.5 mile. From here you get an exquisite view of Lower Falls, a beautiful clear spillway where the water arches over the top ledge and falls in a veil into a shallow pool at least sixty-three feet below.

To return, retrace your steps up the mountainside to your car.

Hinkle Branch Trail

Distance: 1.5 miles
Time: 1.5 hours
Elevation change: 520 feet
Maps: USGS 7½' Camden-on-Gauley
Highlights: Wildflowers, waterfalls, and rapids in Hinkle
   Branch, Cranberry River

Hinkle Branch Trail is a short and very delightful hiking trail in a remote region of the Cranberry River drainage. Hinkle Branch, which parallels the trail, is beautiful during the spring and summer when water is plentiful. The stream tumbles between boulders and down rock slides, and in one place forms a waterfall at least ten feet high. During the spring and summer months, wildflowers are abundant. Orchids, wood sorrel, jack-in-the-pulpit, Indian cucumber-root, trillium, and Solomon's seal are but a few of the jewels growing along the trail.

Another enticing feature for the summer hiker is the Cranberry River at the bottom of the trail. A quick scramble down the riverbank puts you next to a nice secluded swimming hole where more than one hiker has found a wonderful way to cool off when no one was looking!

Hinkle Branch Trail is located near Richwood. To reach the trailhead take WV 39 east from Richwood. Just as you leave the city limits, and one mile west of the Gauley Ranger Station, turn left onto County Route 76. This road is paved. After 2.5 miles, take Forest Service Route 76, which makes a left-hand turn off CR 76. (If you pass a golf course, you have

gone beyond the FS 76 turn.)

Follow the well-maintained gravel FS 76 for an additional 3.6 miles past Woodbine Picnic Area and past the bridge over the Cranberry River to Big Rock Camping Area, where Forest Service Route 81 intersects from the left. FS 81 is not marked, but it is the only major gravel road turning left off FS 76 3.6 miles from the pavement.

Follow FS 81 for 0.7 mile to County Route 7, another unmarked gravel road, which intersects from the left. Turn left onto County Route 7, and drive 1.5 miles to the trailhead. Hinkle Branch crosses CR 7 at the bottom of a little valley, with the road ascending on both sides of the crossing for at least 0.1 mile. The trailhead is located just beyond the double culvert through which Hinkle Branch flows under Route 7. Small pull-offs for parking are on either side of the culvert.

The trailhead is marked only by a Forest Service post on the left side of the road about a hundred feet beyond the culverts. The post looks like a four-foot section of telephone pole stuck in the ground. There is no sign on it. The only other indication that a trail exists here is a yellow blaze on a tree. The trail leaves the road to the left up a small embank-

144 *Southern Mountain Province*

Jack-in-the-pulpit

ment and enters a grove of hemlocks. Blue blazes mark the way as soon as you enter the forest, and the yellow blazes end. Ground pine grows in a thick carpet on the forest floor at the beginning of the path. Birches and maples interspersed with magnolias and hemlocks form the forest canopy. The understory is a mass of ferns, magnolia seedlings, and rhododendron.

Hinkle Branch winds through the forest to the left of the trail for the first fifth of a mile. Then, the path fords Hinkle Branch to parallel the opposite bank for the remainder of the route. It follows an old railroad grade part of the way, as evidenced by the old decayed crossties that have left ridges in the forest floor. Gradu-

ally descending parallel to Hinkle Branch, the path offers numerous views down into the waters of the stream. The largest waterfall is located about 0.4 to 0.5 mile along the trail.

After hiking approximately 0.75 mile, you will intersect with the Cranberry River in a secluded section. The trail ends here. To return to your car, just retrace your steps.

There is no obvious access to the river from the trail. You will have to scramble through rhododendrons down a steep bank to reach the water. This scramble is rewarded with a view of a beautiful stretch of the boulder-lined river where fishing and swimming opportunities abound. The water is crystal clear, making even the deepest pools look deceptively shallow.

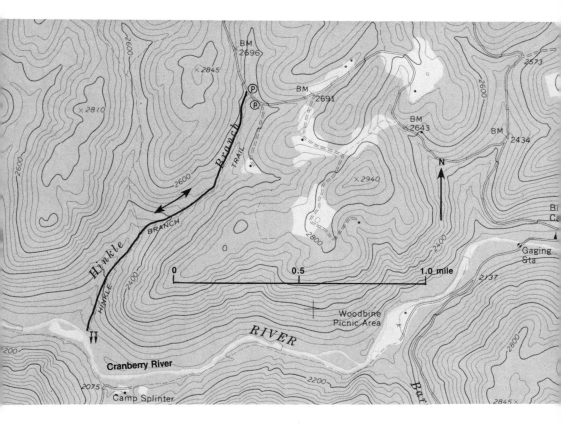

35

Blue Bend Recreation Area

Distance: 6.3 miles
Time: 4 hours
Elevation change: 1,400 feet
Maps: USGS 7½' Anthony
Highlights: Anthony Creek, views

Blue Bend Recreation Area is a beautiful spot in the southern part of the Monongahela National Forest along Anthony Creek. It offers a campground, swimming in Anthony Creek, excellent fishing opportunities, and beautiful hiking trails. The *Hiking Guide to Monongahela National Forest and Vicinity* gives Blue Bend Loop Trail, the hike we describe, the highest rating possible for scenery.

Blue Bend Recreation Area is reached by turning east on Anthony Creek Road from US 219 south of Frankford. After about four miles this road leads through the tiny community of Anthony, then crosses the Greenbrier River Trail and the Greenbrier River and enters the Monongahela National Forest. Ignore all intersecting gravel roads and continue along the paved road to Blue Bend Recreation Area, which is about 4.2 miles beyond the Greenbrier River crossing. Turn right into Blue Bend Recreation Area, and park in the lot near the bathhouses. This portion of Blue Bend Recreation Area is for swimming and picnicking.

Blue Bend Loop Trail begins on the south bank of Anthony Creek downstream from the swimming area. The trailhead is reached by walking through the

picnic area to the footbridge across the creek below the beaches. Take the footbridge across the creek where several trails come together. The second trail from the right is marked with a sign for Blue Bend Loop Trail. Because this is a loop, you may hike the trail in either direction. We describe the hike going down Anthony Creek first, following the rightmost trail, which parallels the stream bank. The trail is blazed in blue. Even though sometimes the blazes are faded and rather far apart, the trail is easy to follow.

Anthony Creek is a joy to walk along during just about any season. It is about twenty to thirty yards wide in the fast sections, which are interrupted by much wider, slow-moving deep pools. The water is so clear that you can see trout swimming near the bottom of the deepest pools. In summer, you can enjoy a refreshing dip in one of these many deeper sections.

In early spring, the wildflowers along Anthony Creek are spectacular. Clintonia, Virginia bluebells, hepatica, and both red and white trillium are but a few of the plants along the trail. Trillium is one of

Mayfly

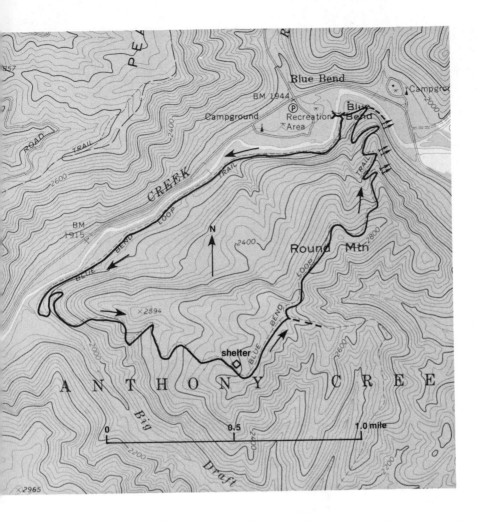

the showier early spring wildflowers. The name is based on the Latin tri, meaning "three," because trilliums have three leaves, and each flower part comes in threes: three sepals, three petals, three stigmas, as well as a three-chambered pistil. Native Indians chewed the underground stems, believing them to cure snakebites. Trillium was also used to stimulate uterine contractions in childbirth and to soothe sore nipples in nursing mothers. Although no longer used in these ways, trilliums tend to suffer from overpicking because of their attractiveness.

Bird watchers will enjoy the diversity of birds along the trail. Louisiana water thrushes bob along the side of Anthony Creek while great crested flycatchers squawk from the treetops. Parula warblers and black-throated green warblers sing throughout the woodland in the spring.

After about 0.9 mile, a big pool is visible through the trees on the opposite bank of the creek. Wild irises and morel mushrooms grow along this section of the trail. Ignore the several ancient overgrown roads that intersect the trail from time to time. These old roads are not easily confused with the main trail, which is well-worn. Continue following the blue-blazed trail along the stream.

After hiking 1.9 miles, you will see a sign for Blue Bend Loop Trail at a trail junction. Turn left at this junction, following the sign. The trail to the right crosses Big Draft, a small tributary of Anthony Creek. This is Anthony Creek Trail, also blue-blazed. If you cross a small creek (Big Draft), you have just missed the left turn for the loop trail.

The trail curves away from Anthony Creek at this left turn and begins ascending Round Mountain paralleling Big Draft for a short distance. The first of several switchbacks is at two miles. At this point, the trail leaves Big Draft, and the vegetation changes abruptly from the moist forest of hemlock along the water's edge to a drier forest of pine and oak on the steep slopes. Another switchback is encountered at 2.25 miles. At 2.3 miles, the path traverses around to the south side of Round Mountain. At 2.8 miles, the trail makes a sharp left and continues up the side of the mountain.

An Adirondack-type shelter with a picnic table is located on the left side of the trail at 3.4 miles. Water is available from a nearby spring except in extremely dry weather. The spring is located just behind and below the shelter to the north.

The path turns into a jeep trail at the shelter and ascends to follow along the crest of Round Mountain. During the winter, nice views can be seen through the trees from the trail along the crest of the mountain. At 3.9 miles, Blue Bend Loop Trail leaves to the left of the jeep trail, becoming a narrow footpath. The trail is level for a while before it descends, leaving the dry forest for moist rhododendron thickets.

At 5.0 miles, the trail curves sharply and offers the first and best of three superb views of Anthony Creek winding through the valley below. From these overlooks, you can see several farms, some of them growing nursery stock. The next overlook is at 5.3 miles, and the last is at 5.7 miles. The trail descends between each overlook. Care must be taken at these overlooks, for they are rock outcrops with steep drops and no guardrails.

The path descends through thick rhododendron brakes to a giant hemlock grove at the valley bottom. Charred stumps along the trail indicate a past fire. Turn left at an intersection at 6.0 miles and follow the path as it passes a picnic shelter on the right with a small path leading to it. The beginning of the loop is intersected at 6.3 miles. Here, retrace your way across the footbridge to your vehicle.

Seneca State Forest

Distance: 6.4 miles
Time: 4 hours
Elevation change: 718 feet
Maps: USGS 7½′ Clover Lick; State Forest map
Highlight: Views

Seneca State Forest is West Virginia's oldest, and second largest, state forest. The 11,684-acre forest is bordered on the west by the Greenbrier River at an elevation of 2,200 feet. At the far eastern edge is Michael Mountain, more than 1,400 feet higher. The hike described here on Crestline Trail will take you to the high eastern part of the forest. Another hike in this book (Hike number 40, Greenbrier River Trail) describes the lower western region.

To reach Seneca State Forest, drive east about five miles from Marlinton on WV 39, and turn north on WV 28 near Huntersville. Follow WV 28 for ten miles to the state forest entrance. From the entrance, go 0.4 mile and turn right onto a dirt road leading to a picnic area. Follow the dirt road one mile to a fork in the road. Take the right fork, and park your car in the pull-out at the Rich Patch Hollow trailhead, which is 0.1 mile past the fork.

You begin your hike by walking on the same dirt road from the parking area. There is no gate to prevent you from driving farther than the pull-out, but the road becomes too rough and steep for ordinary cars beyond that point. The road ascends through a dry, second-growth forest of oak, chestnut (sprouting), pine, and maple. The understory is cloaked in shrubs: blueberry, mountain laurel, and azalea.

Despite its remote location, the state forest, and the region surrounding the Greenbrier River generally, has been radically changed by a history of lumbering. In pre-settlement days, the region was covered with a vast forest of white pine. As with spruce at higher elevations, this valuable conifer soon disappeared before the lumberjack's saw. White pine and spruce have fared poorly in regrowth after lumbering, possibly because they can only reproduce by seed, where many hardwoods will sprout vigorously from the base when cut. This gives the hardwoods a head start in the succession that follows cutting, especially when the seed source for the conifer (the adult trees) has been removed.

The road ascends at a steady pace for 1.2 miles where it reaches a dead end. At the top of the climb is an overgrown side trail leading to a former fire tower site. You can enjoy superb views from the large rock outcrop where the tower sat.

At the roadhead, the trail along the ridgetop is marked with a sign saying

"Crestline Trail." Camping and open fires are not permitted along the trail. At 1.7, 2.2, 2.7, and 3.0 miles, the trail reaches high points on the ridge, and views open to the east or west through the trees. Despite the rocky soil and exposure to strong winds, a number of wildflowers may be seen along the trail in spring and early summer. Wild geranium, perfoliate bellwort, columbine, bristly sarsaparilla, lily-of-the-valley, and pink lady's-slipper may be found here, clinging to protected sites.

From the many vantage points along the trail, if you listen carefully you may hear some guttural, crow-like calls in the distance. Fifty years ago, a bird watcher would have been ecstatic at the sound, for the common raven was all but extinct in the southern mountains of the eastern United States—a victim of ignorance and superstition. The raven has since made a dramatic and welcome comeback, thanks to education and protection of their preferred habitat.

A little observation reveals the raven as a very social bird, not to mention athletic and comical. A family group of ravens,

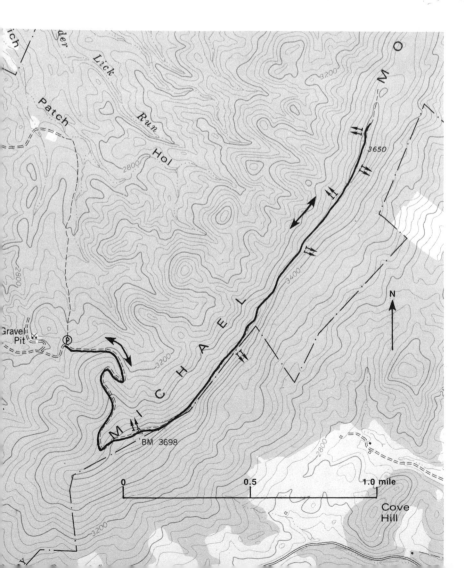

Allegheny menziesia

all swooping, twisting, and diving at each other, makes for an exciting aeronautical display. In one amazing stunt, a bird will fold its wings and momentarily flip upside down in midflight! You have to see this maneuver several times to believe it, but a cavorting group of ravens will quite often oblige. Its intelligence, sociability, and good-natured boisterous behavior all engender a genuine fondness for the raven. The return of this species to our Appalachian peaks is welcome indeed.

At 3.2 miles the highest point of the ridge is reached at an elevation of 3,650 feet. Beyond the peak, the path becomes obscure. From this point, retrace your steps along Crestline Trail to the road-head, and follow the road down to your car.

37

Watoga State Park

Distance: 6.7 miles
Time: 5 hours
Elevation change: 960 feet
Maps: USGS 7½' Denmar; Park map
Highlights: Views, wildflowers

Watoga State Park is the largest, oldest, and one of the most beautiful state parks in the West Virginia state park system. The name of the park comes from the Indian word *watauga*, which means "river of islands." Indeed, the Greenbrier River, which skirts the edge of the park, has a number of islands in it near the park. The 10,000-plus acre park features camping, cabins, a restaurant, swimming, boating, fishing, tennis, and horseback riding. Numerous short hiking trails are available in the park, allowing you to take further advantage of its scenic beauty. You can do the hike described here in about half a day. It takes you along the placid Greenbrier River as well as up to a beautiful overlook of the river valley.

To reach Watoga State Park, turn east onto Seebert Road from US 219 just north of the Pearl S. Buck birthplace near Hillsboro. Seebert Road enters Watoga State Park immediately after crossing the Greenbrier River, 2.4 miles from US 219. Turn right into Riverside Campground 0.7 mile inside the park boundary. Drive to the far eastern edge of the campground, and park near the bathhouse. The hike begins on Jesse's Cove Trail. The trailhead is marked with signs, and the trail itself is blazed in yellow.

Jesse's Cove Trail descends immediately to the east bank of the Greenbrier River. Piles of driftwood and assorted flotsam and jetsam mark the high-water line, which occasionally reaches above the trail. At 0.1 mile the yellow blazes lead you up and away from the river while a fisherman's trail continues along the bank. Soon after, the trail follows an old road, still parallel to the river. The trail veers left away from the road at 0.5 mile. In spring, stands of trillium, jack-in-the-pulpit, and Solomon's seal flank the trail.

The trail bends away from the river at 0.6 mile, following Rock Run to the east away from the Greenbrier. Rock Run is a beautiful little stream surrounded by a lush forest. Numerous species of spring wildflowers can be seen here along with a diverse mixture of tall trees. Black cohosh, violets, wild ginger, Dutchman's-breeches, partridgeberry, lady's-slipper, miterwort, baneberry, foamflower, and sharp-lobed hepatica are but a few of the inhabitants of Jesse's Cove.

The trail crosses the stream at 1.0 mile and recrosses to the north side at 1.2 miles. You hike through a veritable tunnel of rhododendron at 1.4 miles, and then begin ascending away from the stream bottom into a drier habitat. The trail

meets the stream again at 1.7 miles, crossing again at 1.8 and 2.0 miles. These crossings usually are easily accomplished with dry feet by rock-hopping. At 2.2 miles the trail veers away from the stream again and traverses a steep slope above the valley bottom.

Uprooted trees along the side of the trail have left mounds of soil with pits below them where the tree used to stand. These small disturbances in the forest floor create ideal habitats for certain plants to get established. You can even discover certain species that are associated only with the pits and others found only on the mounds. Mounds tend to be rather dry, while pits are relatively wet, so from the plant's point of view, they are two very different habitats. Pits also collect snow in winter, effectively shortening the growing season, while mounds melt off quickly and therefore have a longer growing season.

The trail ascends to a restored cabin at 3.0 miles. A sign nearby explains the century-long history of the cabin. Built in 1887, the house belonged to Andrew Workman and his family, who lived in Jesse's Cove for twenty-five years before pushing on for greener pastures in the Pacific Northwest. The Jarvis family then occupied the site until 1922 when the land was purchased by the state as part of the game refuge that was to become Watoga State Park. Subsistence farming and sales of ginseng sustained both families in this isolated setting. The cabin fell into disrepair after 1939 but was restored by park personnel in 1981.

The trail leaves the clearing of the cabin following an old road up the valley. At 3.2 miles the trail bends right into a drier oak-pine forest with an understory of blueberries. A junction with Ann Bailey Lookout Trail (unblazed) is reached at 3.4 miles. Turn left at this intersection, following a wider dirt road. At 3.9 miles you pass a graveyard containing memorials to some members of the Workman family who died during their stay in Jesse's Cove.

The Ann Bailey Lookout is reached at 5.0 miles. The lookout is an unusual, elevated log structure that you can climb up inside to gain a superb view of the Greenbrier River Valley, the Greenbrier River Trail and farmland beyond in the "Little Levels" region.

No explanation is given at the site for the name of the lookout, but the story of Ann Bailey is well worth recounting. Barbara McCallum, in an article for *Wonderful West Virginia* magazine, portrays Ann as a "hard-riding, fearless pioneer." Shortly after the Revolutionary War, the frontier in West Virginia was still the site of serious conflicts between white settlers and native Americans. Legend has it that Fort Lee (at Charleston) was under siege by Indians in 1789. The defenses at the fort were facing potential disaster at the hands of the Indians because gunpowder supplies were running short. Colonel Clendenin, commander of the fort's garrison, called a meeting and asked for a volunteer to ride the hundred miles to Fort Savannah (at Lewisburg) to secure adequate powder to defend the fort. The room was silent as the brave pioneers contemplated the risk of life and scalp involved. From the back of the room, Ann Bailey spoke up: "I will go."

The swiftest horse was saddled, and Ann was off. One day and a hundred miles later she arrived at Fort Savannah. She successfully returned with a second horse packing the needed powder. As a reward for her bravery, she was given the fast steed by a vote of the garrison. Henceforth, Ann continued to ride between forts, carrying vital information and supplies. She became known as "Mad Ann," not because she actually was mad, but because her risky rides seemed

View from inside Ann Bailey Lookout Tower

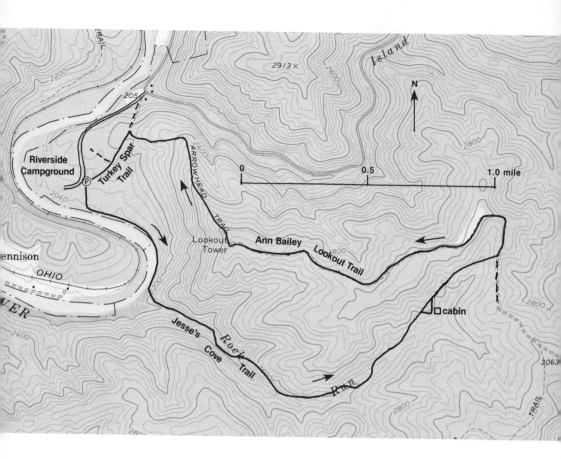

sheer madness to her Indian-shy fellow settlers. Her bravery is now commemorated with a monument at her grave in Tu-Endie-Wei Park at Point Pleasant.

Arrowhead Trail (sparsely blazed in yellow) leaves the clearing of the lookout on the left side. You begin descending a dry ridge below the lookout. At 6.2 miles from the trailhead, you turn left on Turkey Spur Trail to Riverside Campground, while Arrowhead Trail goes straight toward the cabin area. At 6.3 miles a driveway to a water tower leaves Turkey Spur Trail to the left. At 6.5 miles the trail forks. The right fork takes you to the campground office. Your car is 0.2 mile ahead in the campground.

Cow Pasture Trail

Distance: 7.5 miles
Time: 6 hours
Elevation change: 320 feet
Maps: USGS 7½' Hillsboro, Lobelia
Highlights: Views, glades

Cranberry Glades and Cranberry Back-country are two of West Virginia's best-known attractions for outdoor enthusiasts. Cow Pasture Trail takes you through a shrubby section of the glades and then along the border of the backcountry as it encircles the glades. It is a nice, relatively easy day hike with few ups and downs. Parking for this loop trail is located at the Cranberry Glades Botanical Area.

To reach Cranberry Glades Botanical Area, drive east from Richwood on WV 39/150. The spur road (FS 102) to the Botanical Area is a well-marked left turn. The parking lot is 1.5 miles from this turn on the right side of the road.

You begin the hike by walking farther (northwest) along the spur road. At 0.8 mile you reach the end of the road at a parking lot. On the right you will notice signs warning against trespassing in the glades area. Special permission is required to enter the area because the wetlands are notoriously susceptible to damage due to trampling. They can quickly become muddy quagmires, devoid of the interesting plants that make the glades so attractive to visitors. In short, areas such as Cranberry Glades easily could be loved to death.

The road is gated beyond this parking lot. Cow Pasture Trail leaves to the east of the road beyond this gate at 1.0 mile. You are now entering Cranberry Wilderness Area, which is closed to motorized vehicles. The intersection with Cow Pasture Trail is marked with a sign. The blue-blazed trail follows a level, straight railroad grade at the outset. Shortly, the trail enters the lower end of the glades area. There are hemlocks on the higher ground, but alders, a variety of sedges, and mosses flank the trail in low-lying areas. In spots the trail is wet in almost any season of the year. A bridge crosses the small headwater stream of Cranberry River at 1.1 miles. The trail enters an open meadow at 1.2 miles and then crosses through the center of the clearing. Behind you is a clear view of Kennison Mountain (elevation 4,445 feet).

The trail re-enters the woods on the far side of the meadow. On the north side of the glades, the trail alternately passes through open meadows (probably old cow pastures) and woods. This mixture of woods and fields should yield excellent bird watching in spring. At 1.6 miles the trail veers to the right and becomes somewhat obscured by overgrowing weeds. Stay toward the right, remaining above the swampy area, and watch for

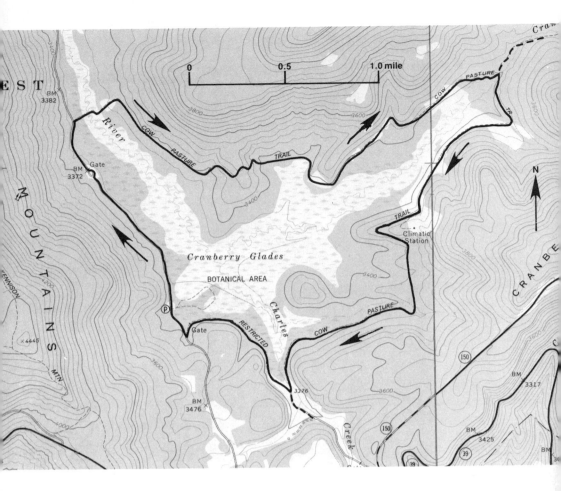

blue blazes marking the trail.

In several of the openings you get nice views to the south toward the high mountain ridges. At 1.9 miles the trail ascends, leveling out in an open meadow. The trail follows the left side of this meadow, climbing once again at 2.0 miles. At 2.1 miles you begin to descend, crossing a small drainage at 2.3 miles. An abandoned beaver dam and house can be seen to the right of the trail in a low area. At 3.2 miles the trail crosses a small, pretty stream. At 3.6 miles the trail enters

View across Cranberry Glades

a large meadow with a good view to the south of a wet meadow and pond. Another stream is crossed at 3.8 miles. Here you can see evidence of recent flooding with piles of washed-up sticks and other natural debris. At 4.0 miles the trail comes to a well-used campsite, with a stream nearby.

The trail is easily lost at 4.2 miles. Notice a large hemlock near the trail with a nearby birch marked by two blue blazes. A false trail leads straight ahead past the hemlock. Turn right at a forty-five-degree angle at the hemlock and you will cross a stream within thirty feet. Then the trail enters an open field and the path becomes more obvious. Nice views open to the north toward the Cranberry Backcountry and Black Mountain (elevation 4,490 feet).

The trail soon meets an old road, which slowly climbs away from the valley bottom. At 5.1 miles the trail enters the woods, still climbing. The trail passes a high point on a ridge and then bends left and begins descending through a lovely mixed hardwood forest. At 6.7 miles the trail enters a glade with a stream (Charles Creek) running through the center of it. The trail stays on the left side. You can see an old beaver dam on the right side of the trail.

Cross over Charles Creek on the top of the old beaver dam, and continue toward a gate with a "road closed" sign near it. Ignore the blue blazes leading straight ahead here and turn right, following FS 980 along the border of the Botanical Area.

Signs once again warn against entering the boggy areas to the right of the road. Tangled masses of rhododendrons along with the deep black muck are enough to discourage most people from taking side trips. At 7.4 miles, the road is gated, then the trail emerges in a large clearing with a campsite. The spur road to the Botanical Area parking lot is a hundred yards ahead. Turn right on the road to return to your car.

Sherwood Lake Recreation Area

Distance: 10.8 miles
Time: 8 hours
Elevation change: 1,160 feet
Maps: USGS 7½' Rucker Gap, Falling Spring, Mountain
  Grove, Lake Sherwood
Highlights: Rhododendron and azalea, views, lake

Sherwood Lake Recreation Area offers many recreational opportunities, including hiking, in a scenic mountain setting in eastern West Virginia. The circuit hike described here follows a stream to the Virginia–West Virginia border, and then follows the border south, offering nice views into Virginia's Lake Moomaw area. Plan to spend a full, enjoyable day on the trail.

To reach Sherwood Lake (also referred to as Lake Sherwood), turn east from WV 92 in Neola onto Sherwood Lake Road near the Anthony Correctional Center. The entrance to the Recreation Area is reached 9.6 miles from this turn, and parking for the circuit hike is available on the right side of the road near a gate just past the entrance to West Shore Campground, 10.5 miles from WV 92. Between Memorial Day and Labor Day the gate is open and you may drive 0.4 mile farther to a second parking area along this road by the trailhead, just past the entrance to Pine Run Campground on a loop in the road. We list mileages starting at the trailhead by the second parking area.

The hike begins on Snake Valley Trail. About a hundred yards from the trailhead, another trail crosses Snake Valley Trail. You go straight ahead across the trail intersection. At 0.2 and 0.5 mile the trail crosses small streams. Near the second stream an unmarked trail comes in from the right. You continue straight ahead here too.

The trail meets and follows Meadow Creek at 0.7 mile. Meadow Creek is a picturesque stream about ten feet wide at this elevation. It winds through an open oak and pine forest, but along the banks a deep shade is cast by the evergreen hemlock and rhododendron. You will pass an area where beavers have dammed the creek along here.

The trail fords the stream at 0.9 mile and, depending on the water level, you may have to wade across. On the far side of the creek, the trail enters a tangle of shrubby heath plants, including two species of rhododendron, mountain laurel, Allegheny menziesia, blueberries, trailing arbutus, and teaberry. Take away the trees, and you could easily be on Dolly Sods at an elevation of 4,000 feet.

The two species of rhododendron are very similar when the plants are not in flower, but catawba rhododendron (also known as mountain rosebay or purple laurel) has lilac-purple flowers, while great laurel (or just rhododendron) has white to light pink flowers. When they are not

Spillway of Sherwood Lake Dam

flowering you can distinguish them by the long appendages, or scales, surrounding the terminal buds of great laurel. Catawba rhododendron lacks these long scales. The two species grow side-by-side along Meadow Creek, but if you observe carefully you may note that catawba rhododendron is found in slightly drier sites. They remain genetically isolated from one another in part by a difference in flowering time. Catawba rhododendron flowers in May or early June, while great laurel blooms in late June or early July. The result of this isolation is not only two distinct species, but also a tremendous flower show along this valley through much of late spring and early summer.

Snake Valley Trail crosses Meadow Creek ten times in the next three miles,

each crossing becoming a little easier as the stream gets smaller the higher you go. A trail junction is reached at 3.8 miles. To the left is an access trail to Meadow Mountain Trail. Snake Valley Trail continues to the right onto a fire trail marked with blue blazes, and you follow it.

At 3.9 miles, the fire road veers to the right while the blue blazes continue straight ahead. Follow the blue-blazed trail. In short order the trail enters a clearing (about one acre) with fenced young trees in it. On the far side of the clearing a sign points the way to Allegheny Mountain Trail. You intersect Allegheny Mountain Trail and the Virginia–West Virginia border at 4.3 miles. Turn right here, now guided by red blazes.

The trail ascends the ridge, eventually reaching an elevation of 3,214 feet. Much of the trail stays above 3,000 feet,

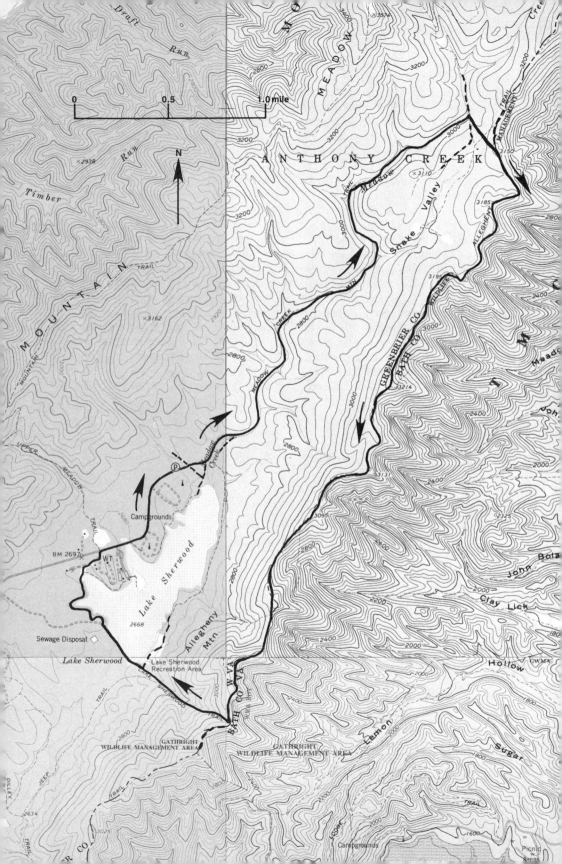

so there is no distinct summit. The trail climbs and descends gently, remaining on the ridgetop for the next four miles. Occasional views through the trees reveal a steep drop into Virginia to the east. Before turning toward Sherwood Lake you can see Lake Moomaw through the trees 1,500 vertical feet below you. Beyond the lake are more high ridges of the George Washington National Forest.

The trail reaches a junction where you turn right onto Virginia Trail at 8.4 miles in a saddle on the ridge. Virginia Trail takes you back to Sherwood Lake, closely following the route that early settlers who had farms along Meadow Creek used to reach a Virginia store. The trail descends rapidly, reaching a wooden bridge at 8.6 miles. Near the bridge an unmarked trail joins Virginia Trail from the right, and a sign erroneously identifies the trail you are walking as Lake Sherwood Trail. At 8.8 miles a similar incorrect sign is reached.

The real intersection with Sherwood Lake Trail is reached at 9.0 miles, and you turn left, following Sherwood Lake Trail toward the lower end of the lake. The trail passes below the dam, fords the outlet stream (Meadow Creek), and then winds back up to the levee at the southern end of the lake. Nice views of the lake and surrounding mountains are found on the top of the levee.

You take a grassy road to the end of the levee (at 9.4 miles), and then follow an arrow pointing to the path along the shoreline. The trail parallels the shore around two cattail-lined bays. Past the second bay, you cross a grassy field (unmarked) to a road near a picnic area, then follow this road to the right. Turn left toward the exit at the intersection with another gravel road, then turn right on the main road through the recreation area, reaching your car at 10.8 miles.

Greenbrier River Trail

Distance: 20.8 miles
Time: 2 to 3 days
Elevation change: 240 feet
Maps: USGS 7½′ Edray, Clover Lick, Marlinton; Greenbrier
  River Hike, Bike and Ski Trail, Inc., map
Highlights: River, Sharp's Tunnel and Bridge

The Greenbrier River Trail is a seventy-five mile long trail winding through the Allegheny Mountains beside the pristine Greenbrier River. This trail follows the path of what was once the Greenbrier Division of the C&O Railroad, which was built at the turn of the century to serve the booming lumber industry in this area. Now the rails and ties are gone, and the trail is closed to motorized vehicles, so the nearly level track is perfect for hikers, bikers, and cross-country skiers seeking the solitude and beauty of the West Virginia mountains and rivers.

The section of the Greenbrier described here is probably the most wild and remote section of the trail. It begins in Marlinton and courses 20.8 miles northeast to Sitlington. Isolated stretches where the trail is sandwiched between the peaks of Marlin, Thorny Creek, and Thomas Mountains and the Greenbrier River are interspersed with pastoral scenes of small farms and the sleepy villages of Clover Lick and Stony Bottom. At one point a bridge across the Greenbrier leads the hiker into the side of a mountain through Sharp's Tunnel. Here, you are first treated to an unsurpassed view of the river, then plunged into the darkness of the mountain until your eyes

adjust to bring the light at the other end of the tunnel into perspective.

Overnight accommodations are numerous and varied enough to be suited to all trail users. For the backpacker, there are undeveloped campsites along the trail next to the river. For the day hiker, there are hotels in Marlinton or campgrounds at nearby Watoga State Park and Seneca State Forest. The overnight accommodations that come most highly recommended are those offered by the Elk River Touring Center located on Gil and Mary Willis's farm in nearby Slatyfork. Their farmhouse and cabin is equipped to sleep twenty-one people. You can enjoy Mary's home-cooked meals as you sit around a long farmhouse table with Mary and Gil and the other guests basking in the heat of the woodstove and reflecting on adventures had and yet to be had. Mary will pack you a special lunch for the trail.

The Willises rent cross-country ski equipment and bikes, including the increasingly popular mountain bikes. Numerous guided tours are available, some of which include the Greenbrier River Trail. Gil is very accommodating when it comes to setting up a shuttle for your Greenbrier River Trail excursion. For

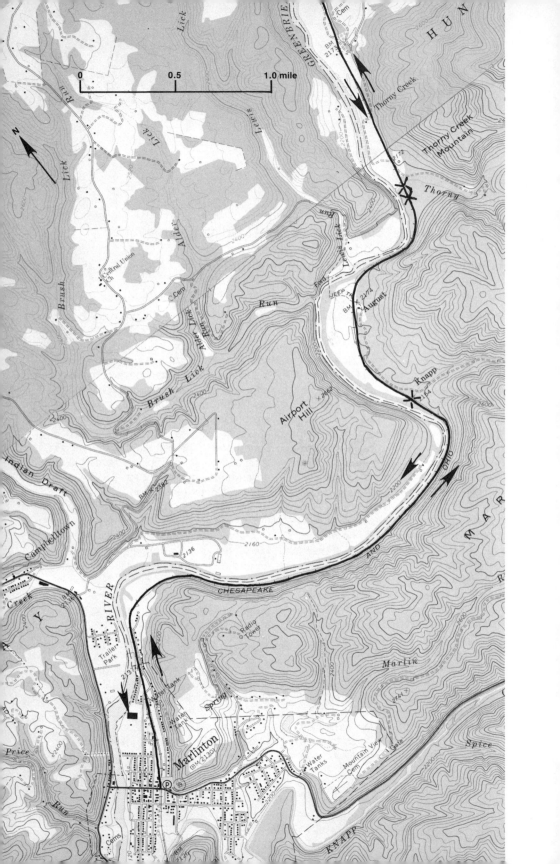

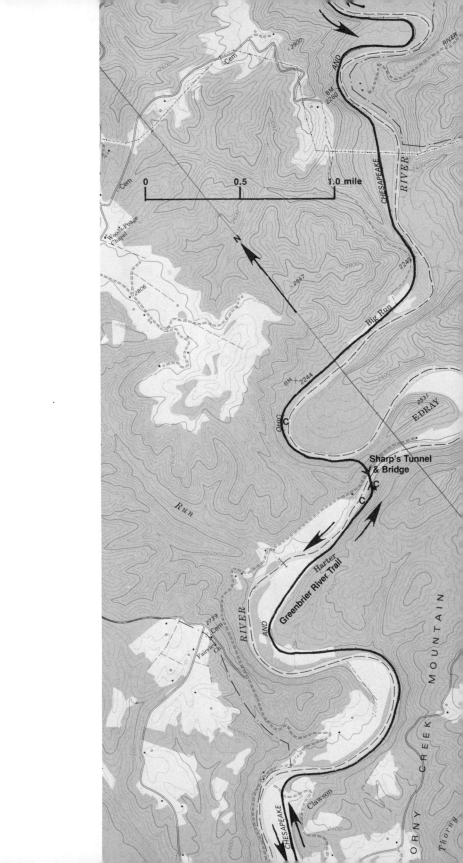

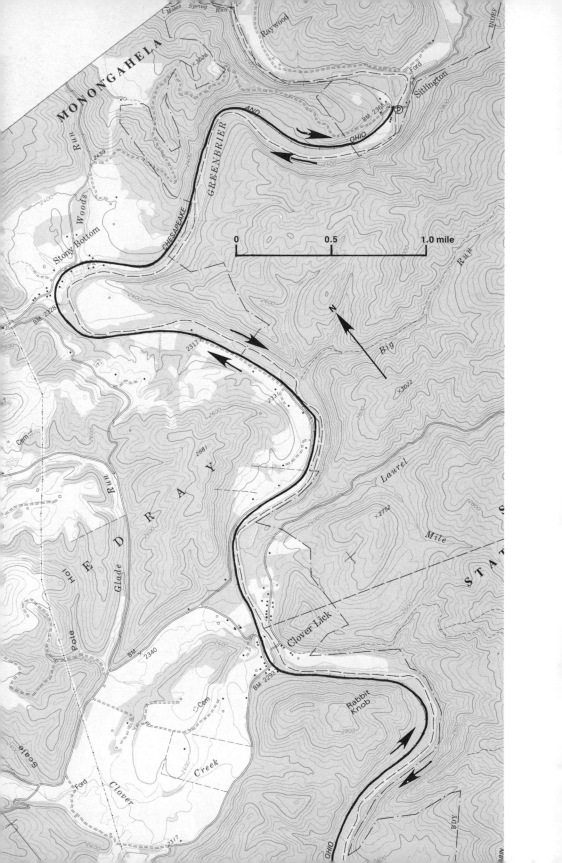

a wonderful homey and relaxing experience, including good food and a good night's sleep—whether it be before or after a day of hiking, biking, or cross-country skiing the Greenbrier River Trail, downhill skiing at nearby Snowshoe, or visiting the nearby Cass Scenic Railway—the Elk River Touring Center is a must.

The trailhead for the section of the Greenbrier River Trail described here is located in Marlinton on the north side of WV 39 (Main Street at Fourth Avenue). Parking is available at the restored railroad depot. A sign next to the depot marks the Greenbrier River Trail, which starts along a section of railroad track with several old restored traincars parked beside the depot. The trail heads north through the back portions of Marlinton by the Home Center and off into the hills. Although numerous small farm access roads cross the trail, there is never any question which is the Greenbrier River Trail. It is very well-marked with signs along the entire route.

Outside Marlinton you will encounter milepost number 57. This is one of the few old railroad mileposts still standing. The mileposts are white unmarked square pillars of cement about four feet high. During the second mile, the trail courses through the back fields of small farms. In places, the trail sidles right up next to the river with the mountainside coming down in cliffs on the right side of the trail. These cliffs are overgrown with hemlocks, rhododendrons, sensitive ferns, dutchman's pipe, and wild raspberries. Sycamores with their striking white bark, alders, river birch, and numerous other moisture-loving plants are found growing along the river bank.

The river offers good fishing as well as boating in an idyllic setting. This section is calm and thus well suited for family canoeing. The water is crystal clear and reportedly clean enough to drink.

Skeleton of a white oak leaf

Soon after the third milepost (59) is a small railroad bridge across a tiny tributary of the Greenbrier, then a more remote section with few signs of humanity. After five miles, you will come upon a flattened cement post bearing a "W" followed by a pair of bridges. These bridges cross Thorny Creek, a major tributary of the Greenbrier.

Pileated woodpeckers, blue jays, flickers, crows, vultures, goldfinches, and rose-breasted grosbeaks are but a few of the fall birds seen along the trail. The varied habitats along the trail promise excellent early morning birding.

No mile posts are encountered for three miles until milepost 63. During this three-mile section, the trail leads through more back fields of small farms. The less-cultivated fields have been invaded by buttonbush, goldenrod, sumac, clematis, milkweed, and gentian.

Mileposts 64 and 65 are still standing. Just beyond milepost 65 is the huge bridge across the Greenbrier leading into Sharp's Tunnel. A bit of flat land between the river and the trail just south of the bridge offers a possible campsite. Above the bridge to the north are more potential riverside campsites. Camping is permitted along the entire trail within fifty feet of the center of the trail on either side as long as you do not camp on the trail or within sight of a road crossing.

The trail curves high above the river on the south side, then crosses the river on Sharp's Bridge. The views of the river both to the east and to the west from the bridge are superb. Below the bridge you may see fish swimming in the current or resting in the quieter eddies.

Just beyond Sharp's Bridge is Sharp's Tunnel. Here the trail plunges into the dark interstices of the mountain for 511 feet to emerge on the west side of the river.

The section of trail between Sharp's Tunnel and the small village of Clover Lick is particularly pretty. To the right of milepost 66 is a nice campsite just before a small bridge crossing a tributary. This site is close to the river and beside the tributary. All along, there are numerous potential campsites between the trail and the river. The mountainsides come down to meet the trail on the left side and the river flows through deep forests on the right side.

At milepost 71, the bridge piers from the old Raine Lumber Company (1913-1929) can be seen in the river. Soon after, a bridge where unmarked County Route 1 crosses the Greenbrier comes into view, and the trail enters Clover Lick, named for the lush fields of clover and the salt licks common here. The town consists of some semi-Victorian houses and other assorted buildings amidst sprawling farms, all in a setting of meadows and trees. The Greenbrier River divides the town.

The sleepy little village once was widely known as a stopping point for those emigrating to Kentucky and Ohio from Maryland, Pennsylvania, and other northeast points. It was favored because the trails from the east avoided the hollows and ravines and followed the high ridges, offering more security from Indian attacks.

As the trail leaves Clover Lick, CR 1 parallels it for part of the way on the left side as it winds its way along the Greenbrier for 3.3 miles to the little village of Stony Bottom. Stony Bottom, like Clover Lick, is a small, rural community in an idyllic setting. Because of its rustic charm, the town has not become run-down despite the demise of the railroad. Many of the houses in Stony Bottom are now vacation homes or camps used primarily during the summer months.

The trail from Stony Bottom to Sitlington is in a relatively remote section. The trail parallels the river around two large bends before arriving in Sitlington. Here County Route 12 from Dunmore crosses the trail and leads across a bridge over the river to Sitlington itself, which is on the east bank.

The point where the road crosses the trail marks the end of this hike. The trail also continues on to Cass, but from Sitlington to Cass, the railroad ties are still in place. Vehicle access here is via CR 12 from Dunmore, which is now the northernmost vehicle crossing on the trail. Parking is possible at the intersection of CR 12 and the trail, but do not intrude on the property of nearby homeowners.

Ridge and Valley Province

41

Swallow Falls State Park

Distance: 1.25 miles
Time: 1 1/2 hours
Elevation change: 120 feet
Maps: USGS 7½' Oakland, Sang Run; Park map
Highlights: Falls, fossils

Swallow Falls State Park is located in the far western part of Maryland, north of Oakland. Situated along the Youghiogheny River, it offers scenic trails through the Youghiogheny Canyon past a number of waterfalls. Between Swallow Falls State Park and nearby Herrington Manor State Park, Garrett State Forest, and Deep Creek Lake State Park, visitors can find numerous recreational possibilities, including camping, boating, cross-country skiing, swimming, hunting, and fishing. In addition, during the summer, nature and history programs are offered daily at Swallow Falls State Park. The hike described here is a short, scenic walk that is perfect for hikers of almost any ability.

Swallow Falls State Park is reached most easily by taking Swallow Falls Road west from US 219 following the signs. This turn goes off US 219 4.3 miles south of the well-marked access road to Deep Creek Lake State Park. Follow Swallow Falls Road 1.3 miles as it passes the Swallow Falls Inn and crosses the Youghiogheny River; then turn right into Swallow Falls State Park. Drive 0.5 mile to a parking lot on the northwest side of

Falls on Muddy Creek

the road opposite Muddy Creek Trail. Signs in the lot point the way to Muddy Creek Falls and Swallow Falls.

The trailhead is across the road from the parking lot. A sign on the edge of the woods along the trail points to Swallow Falls to the right and Muddy Creek to the left. Turn left toward Muddy Creek along the gravel Muddy Creek Trail through the hemlock forest. The trail parallels the park road for a short distance, then turns right away from the road beside a gate preventing vehicle access to the trail. This portion of the trail is paved. From here, you can hear Muddy Creek Falls. The path descends along a moderate grade through lush forests of huge hemlock trees. Ignore an unmarked path intersecting from the left, and continue to the next left across from a trail map sign. This left turn leads along a gravel path to Muddy Creek Falls, which is within view of the turn.

At the top of the falls, a rock ledge allows you to look down over the waterfall to watch the water tumble to the pool below. Wooden steps winding down the steep slope beside the falls let you experience close and moist, blustery views of the falls almost within reach beside you as you descend.

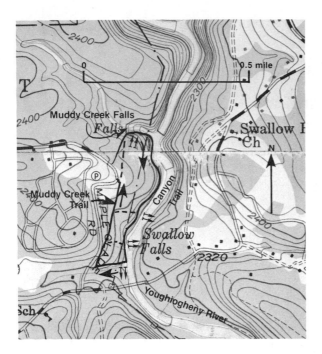

The trail continues downstream from the base of the falls along Muddy Creek, wild with whitewater as it tumbles down a steep boulder-strewn slope. To the right of the trail is a rhododendron-covered cliff. Fossils of plants may be found in the rocks along the creek.

After hiking for about 0.3 mile, you will reach the confluence of Muddy Creek and the Youghiogheny River. A short flight of wooden stairs leads up a slight grade under a huge rock face on the right while the river races below the trail to the left. This is Canyon Trail, which levels out at the top of the stairs and wanders among huge boulders nestled deep in the hemlock forest. The path is well-traveled, and visitors have worn many side trails to the river's edge. The rocks along the trail are great places for children to play.

About 0.5 mile from the trailhead, you will see Lower Falls, a six-foot waterfall. Upstream from Lower Falls and within

view is the larger Swallow Falls. If you happen to be hiking the trail at the right time, you may see kayakers trying their skills in staying upright as they paddle the frothing heavy waters of Lower Falls. A ledge beside Lower Falls at 0.6 mile allows you to look down on Lower Falls or upriver to Swallow Falls, a very pretty view from this point. More imprints of woody plants may be found embedded in the rock.

The trail continues upriver from Lower Falls past intersections with two paths, one at 0.75 mile and the other shortly thereafter. These paths leave to the right of the main trail and connect Canyon Trail with Muddy Creek Trail. Although Swallow Falls is said to be runnable in a kayak, few people would dare try it. Most visitors would prefer to enjoy looking at it safely from a short distance while standing on dry land.

The path curves to the right, away from Swallow Falls to follow along the north bank of Toliver Creek. Toliver Creek forms a small picturesque waterfall a short distance up the trail. At 0.9 mile, follow Muddy Creek Trail, which now turns away from Toliver Creek to the right and leads up a set of railroad-tie steps. From here, the path wanders through the hemlock forest among carpets of wood sorrel.

This wildflower, often called wood shamrock because of the clover-like shape of its leaves, grows in large colonies in the cool dampness of the hemlocks. Its delicate five-petaled white flowers with deep pink veins can be admired between May and August. Because it usually blooms between Easter and Pentacost Sunday in Europe, it is called the Hallelujah Flower. In the United States, however, it is better known for its slightly sour-tasting leaves, which add a touch of interest to a green salad.

Ignore the two trails leading from Muddy Creek Trail back down to Canyon Trail, and continue straight. At 1.25 miles, you will intersect with the parking lot access trail, where you turn left to return to your car.

Seneca Rocks

Distance: 2.7 miles
Time: 2 hours
Elevation change: 840 feet
Maps: USGS 7 1/2′ Upper Tract
Highlights: Cliffs, view

The cliffs forming Seneca Rocks are awe-inspiring. Although these rocks are not part of the highest mountain in West Virginia, this jagged peak is probably the most photographed, the most climbed, and the most respected mountain in this state of mountains. The sheer, naked immensity of the thin bare rock slabs erupting from the deeply forested mountainside is breathtaking.

Residents of the area tell an Indian legend about them. Snowbird, a handsome Indian maiden and daughter of a Seneca chief, loved the cliffs, which she used as her childhood playground. She had learned the footholds and handholds and could scale their sheer face with ease. When it was time to marry, she had seven suitors, but she could not decide which to marry. She scaled the cliffs saying the first brave who could follow her to the top would be the one she would marry. The seven braves attempted the perilous climb. One by one, each failed and fell to his death. The seventh brave was an arm's length from Snowbird when he lost his grip and began to fall. Snowbird quickly reached out and grabbed him, saving his life. This brave she chose as her husband.

If you look closely at the cliffs as you stand in the valley, you can see Snowbird standing alone in a dip in the rocks near the summit waiting for her suitors. Nature has left a monument to her in the form of a tall, narrow slab of sandstone perched apart from the rest.

Mountain climbers rate Seneca Rocks as the most challenging climb in the East. During World War II the Army trained soldiers on the face of the cliffs. The pitons they left behind can still be found in the rock. While the site is still used for military training, more frequently you will see avid weekend mountain climbers scaling the rock face. At the base of the cliffs is a visitors' center with a large glass window facing the cliffs. Soft chairs are lined up in front of the window, where from here the less adventurous can enjoy the adventures of others.

Fortunately for those of us who are not expert rock climbers, there is an alternative route to the spectacular view from the top of Seneca Rocks. The trail is challenging to the lungs, heart, and leg muscles as is any steep climb.

Seneca Rocks is located about eighteen miles southwest of Petersburg on WV 28. The modern visitors' center is lo-

Seneca Rocks

cated below the rocks to the east of the road. You can reach the trailhead by turning east off WV 28 just south of the visitors' center and just beyond the bridge across Seneca Creek onto a tiny dirt road called Roy Gap Road. (This turnoff is immediately north of the junction where US 33 turns west off WV 28.)

The trailhead is 0.2 mile down Roy Gap Road where the road becomes impassable to conventional vehicles. Parking is available in a large area beside the road. To the right of the parking area, a rocky jeep trail leads toward a swinging footbridge across the North Fork of the South Branch of the Potomac River. Cross the footbridge, and turn left on the far side of the river, following the jeep trail. This area is intensively used by visitors. Nevertheless, birds such as the Tennessee warbler, parula warbler, cerulean warbler, and the red-eyed vireo can be seen and heard along the route. Wildflowers such as wild geranium, bloodroot, violets, and horsetails line the jeep track.

A sign at about 0.5 mile reads: "Sene-ca Rocks. You are entering a natural area with hazards associated with rocks and high places. In using this area, you should be properly trained, equipped and physically fit. You are responsible for your own safety and the protection of others. Preserve and protect the area. It is not indestructible."

Although this sign is directed to rock climbers, it carries a message for all users. The jeep trail continues ascending the moderate slope along the south bank of a small creek. At 0.6 mile is a memorial rock dedicated to a rock climber who died in a fall here. Just beyond this memorial, the road fords the creek.

At 0.7 mile, a sign to the left of the road points to routes to the east side and North Peak, which are for rock climber use only. Just beyond this sign at 0.75 mile are two wooden posts and rock steps leading upslope toward a snow fence. Trees blazed in yellow and red are additional signals. This is the footpath to the top. Turn left off the jeep road, and take the steep footpath following the yel-

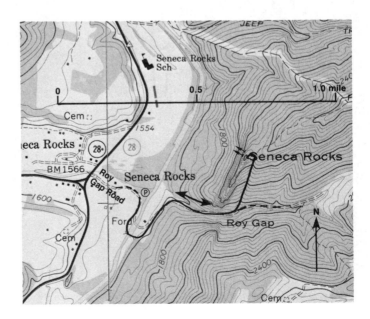

low blazes. The trail is very, very steep, and the terrain is a jumble of rocks. Yet, the only requirements for hiking this trail are that you know your physical limits, and that you have the stamina and will power to forge ahead despite aching muscles and burning lungs.

At 0.9 mile, you will come to a narrow knife of rock pointing straight up. Go to the right of this, following the yellow arrows. At 1.15 miles, the path divides. Either route leads to the same destination, and they reunite at a saddle in the ridge just behind the cliffs. When you gain the ridge, be sure to follow the yellow blazes along the ridgetop to the cliffs, ignoring all other paths that descend from the ridge. At 1.25 miles stand a couple of signs noting severe erosion on a number of old trails. Be sure to heed the signs; stay off these paths to give them a chance to recover.

The last section of the trail is not for unsupervised children or for those afraid of heights. The trail leads to the top of the rock outcrop where you must pick your way carefully around and between the rocks to gain the unfenced summit of Seneca Rocks. From this narrow perch, you look down over the valley formed by the North Fork of the South Branch of the Potomac River. Before you spreads a vast expanse of farmland and forests, with the river winding through the bottomland. Beyond the valley, mountain after mountain can be seen fading into the distant haze. Farther up and down this same mountain range are other outcroppings of the Seneca Rock formation.

On the way up the trail, you may have asked yourself what could be worth the exertion of the steep climb. The spectacular view is your answer.

To return to the trailhead, retrace your steps, breathing more easily on the way down.

Cacapon State Park: Ziler Loop Trail

Distance: 4.1 miles
Time: 2 1/2 hours
Elevation change: 1,040 feet
Maps: USGS 7½' Ridge, Great Cacapon, Park map
Highlights: Views of Shenandoah Valley

Cacapon State Park is located on WV 522, eighteen miles south of US 40 and ten miles south of Berkeley Springs in the eastern panhandle of West Virginia. The park sits at the base of Cacapon Mountain, which is one part of a long ridge in the "ridge and valley province" east of the Allegheny Mountains. This area of West Virginia and adjacent states has sharply folded rock strata that form long parallel "waves" of ridges. The ridge and valley province contrasts with most of West Virginia's mountains, which while folded are much less regular in pattern. Cacapon State Park has a golf course, a lodge and cabins, and a lake for boating and swimming, in addition to the usual picnic areas and playgrounds. At over 6,000 acres, it is one of the state's largest state parks, and much of the acreage remains in its natural wild state.

The Ziler Loop Trail is reached by following signs to the Batt Picnic Area from the park entrance. The trail begins at the north end of the parking lot farthest to the east at the picnic area. Initially, you follow a jeep road for less than 200 feet. The trail is marked with red and blue blazes, and it turns left off the jeep road. Within the next 500 feet is an intersection with Central Trail (red blazes), which

forks right from Ziler Loop Trail. You continue straight, following red and blue blazes.

As you begin to ascend Cacapon Mountain, you may notice many leafless, or mostly leafless, trees in the forest. These trees are dead or dying as the result of infestation by loopers (moth larvae). These larvae or "inchworms" have eaten the foliage from the trees for several years in succession, causing the death of the weaker trees. Loopers are not the only pests plaguing this forest. Gypsy moths are also a menace. Although the gypsy moth is a new arrival to West Virginia, foresters are worried that its rapid southwestern migration may result in widespread forest devastation. Research is currently underway concerning the ecological effects of this pest and how it might be controlled. You may see pieces of cloth wrapped around some of the trees near Ziler Loop Trail. These "skirts" are designed to lure gypsy moth larvae as they descend the tree trunk in search of cover. The larvae hide beneath the skirts where they can be counted to estimate population size.

At the next intersection (0.4 mile), the

White-tailed deer

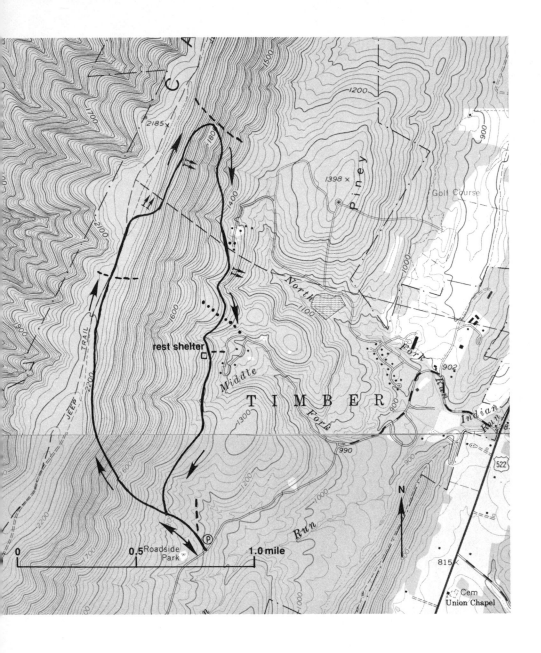

return route of Ziler Loop Trail (red and blue blazes) comes in from the right. Take the left fork, following the blue blazes. The trail steadily rises through dry woods of chestnut, oak, hickory, and sassafras, with an understory of flowering dogwood. The path ascends to the top of the ridge at an elevation of 2,200 feet. The ridge is flat and densely forested, without a conspicuous summit. As in much of West Virginia, the deer population is probably large, as indicated by a distinct browse line below which there are no green leaves on the trees.

On the ridgetop, the Ziler Trail, marked with orange blazes, crosses Ziler Loop Trail. Follow the blue blazes straight ahead. After following the ridge crest for 0.75 mile, the trail bends right, traversing down the mountain slope through a laurel thicket. As you descend, occasional openings in the forest afford excellent views toward the north end of the Shenandoah Valley. Through a series of switchbacks you descend rapidly. Within 0.5 mile of the switchbacks, the path turns south and makes one long traverse back toward the picnic area. You join a horse trail on this traverse and eventually leave it, following the red and blue blazes of the Ziler Loop Trail to the right.

The trail crosses several seasonal streams on the traverse, but none should be relied upon for drinking water. The Ziler Trail (orange blazes) again crosses Ziler Loop Trail on its way up to the ridgetop, and you continue straight ahead at this junction. After crossing one small stream, you ascend to a rest shelter on the side of the trail. At this point a blue-blazed trail leading south to a group of cabins joins the red-and-blue Ziler Loop Trail. Watch for an abrupt right bend in the Ziler Loop Trail at this point, and continue following the red and blue blazes. You then rejoin the original trail, going left toward the Batt Picnic Area parking lot and your car.

Wolf Gap Recreation Area: Big Schloss

Distance: 4.4 miles
Time: 3 hours
Elevation Change: 1,100 feet
Maps: USGS 7½' Wolf Gap
Highlights: Views

A hike to Big Schloss would be the highlight of any weekend. This trail offers some of the most extensive views to be found in West Virginia. Aside from the exhilarating views of vast forests that it gives you, the peak of Big Schloss is an immense rock outcrop that makes a worthwhile destination in and of itself. For those on a tight budget, a weekend outing with overnight camping in Wolf Gap Recreation Area is free except for gas and food.

Wolf Gap Recreation Area is located on the Virginia–West Virginia border between Winchester and Harrisonburg, Virginia. From I-81 at Woodstock, Virginia, take VA 42 west toward Columbia Furnace for about seven miles where you turn right on County Route 675. Go 6.6 miles on CR 675 to Wolf Gap Recreation Area on the east side of the road.

Wolf Gap is a small rustic camping and picnic area. The area is user-maintained, meaning that no trash cans are provided, and you must pack out what you pack in. The facilities include pit toilets and water from pumps. In 1985, the recreation area was spotless, indicating the respect of the visitors for such a facility. Let's hope it remains this way and continues to provide a refreshing cost-free

adventure for all its visitors.

The trailhead to Big Schloss is between campsites #8 and 9. Parking is available in the parking area opposite the picnic grounds. The trail, marked only with a hiker sign and blazed in yellow, is called Mill Mountain Trail.

At the start, the path is a wide, rocky jeep track ascending the mountain. Ignore the numerous small footpaths leading to various campsites. Blueberries, azalea, and trailing arbutus abound in the understory of the oak and hickory forest. Although you might not see it at first, trailing arbutus may draw your attention by its spicy fragrant flowers during early spring. This tiny plant nestles in the leaf litter along the banks of the path. The waxy, bell-shaped flowers grow in clusters among the leathery evergreen leaves. The ends of each tubular flower flare so that, together, the flowers form sprays of pinkish-white stars.

Trailing arbutus has a firm hold in early American history. Early poets claim that this flower was the earliest to bloom and greet the Pilgrims during their first spring in New England. It is the state flower of

Bridge over rock crevice
on Big Schloss

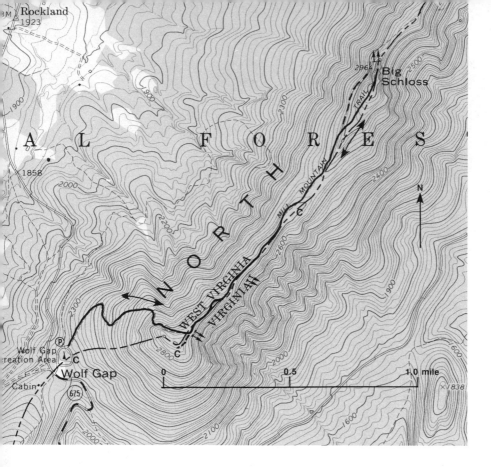

Massachusetts. Indians used it as an astringent, and pioneer doctors used it as a diuretic.

The trail ascends along a moderate slope to the ridge crest at 0.9 mile. A seldom-used path leads along the ridge crest to the right, but Mill Mountain Trail turns left and follows the ridge. A campsite with a rock fire pit is found at this intersection. Just to the right of this campsite, you may catch a glimpse of a view through the trees into Virginia.

Turn left along Mill Mountain Trail, and follow the ridge crest. One mile along the trail, the forest opens up around a rock outcrop on the right side of the trail, yielding a spectacular view into Virginia. Another similar view is found at 1.1 miles. Views of West Virginia are frequent to the left side of the path.

The trail wanders through blueberries in quantities to satisfy any hiker's hunger during August (these berries have been known to pacify toddlers in backpacks for hours). In addition, blackberries grow in several spots along the ridgetop. Cherries, flowering spurge, wild honeysuckle, woodland sunflower, and corydalis also line the path.

Another ridgetop campsite with a rock fire pit is located at 1.5 miles on the right side of the trail. Beyond this site at 1.9 miles, the trail to Big Schloss leaves to the east of Mill Mountain Trail. This short spur is blazed in white and ascends to the top of the rocks forming the peak of

Big Schloss, while Mill Mountain Trail goes below them. Turn left, following the white blazes, and take the narrow, rocky path first to a campsite nestled in the rocks to the left of the path. Beyond this, the trail leads on to the first spectacular overlook, and then on to the last and most spectacular overlook at 2.2 miles.

A rough log bridge spans a deep crevice in the rocks between the first and second overlook. Crossing the bridge on a windy day is an exhilarating experience—there is nothing but rushing air on all sides of you. This overlook is not safe for unattended children. Care must be taken by all, as there are no guardrails to keep you from slipping over the edge of the cliffs.

Big Schloss is 2,964 feet above sea level, offering nearly a 360–degree view. On a clear day you can see far into both Virginia and West Virginia. Looking east into Virginia, you can see across Stony Creek to Little Sluice Mountain and Little Schloss at an elevation of 2,624 feet. Toward the west into West Virginia is an outstanding view of Trout Run Valley and Long Mountain. Most of the land visible from this lookout is in the George Washington National Forest, which makes this view a rare treat. There are few areas in Virginia or West Virginia with views of such extensive, unbroken forest.

To return to your vehicle, retrace your steps to Wolf Gap Recreation Area.

Savage River State Forest: Monroe Run Trail

Distance: 4.5 miles
Time: 3 hours
Elevation change: All downhill
Maps: USGS 7½' Bittinger; State Forest map
Highlight: Monroe Run

Monroe Run Trail is an easy downhill hike from Meadow Mountain along Monroe Run to a campground in Big Run State Park. Located in the extensive Savage River State Forest, this hike makes an enjoyable afternoon or morning outing along a sparkling mountain stream rushing over boulders and ledges in its descent to the Savage River Reservoir.

Although we describe this hike as a one-way trip with a pickup vehicle at the bottom, a day hike up Monroe Run and back, using the campground as a base, would be equally enjoyable. To reach the campground at Big Run State Park, take Exit 19 off Interstate 48 at Grantsville, and head north on MD 495. Turn right (east) at 0.7 mile onto US 40 (Alt). You will reach New Germany Road 2.2 miles from this junction. Turn right (south) on New Germany Road toward New Germany State Park and Big Run State Park. At 5.8 miles from this intersection, a sign marks the point where the road enters Savage River State Forest.

Watch for a left turn on Big Run Road toward Big Run State Park 5.4 miles from the state forest border. One mile from this turnoff, Big Run Road becomes gravel. Five miles from the turnoff, the gravel

road intersects Savage River Road. At this intersection is the entrance to the campground. Park your pickup vehicle near the end of the trail at campsites #5 and 6.

To reach the trailhead, retrace your route up Big Run Road to New Germany Road, where you turn left. Monroe Run Trail is 2.75 miles to the southwest of this intersection. If you pass Monroe Run Vista, you have gone 0.2 mile beyond the trailhead. Parking is possible along the shoulder of the road at the trailhead.

The trail is marked by a sign informing the public that this is a hiking trail only and that no motorized vehicles are allowed. The trail begins as an undeveloped dirt road along a power line through an area that has been selectively logged recently. A few oaks and maples are still standing. The trail turns right, away from the disturbed area, and enters mature woods at 0.1 mile. The path is grassy and seems rarely used. It descends a slight grade through a forest of maple, birch, oak, and sassafras.

The sassafras tree is one of the easiest trees to remember. Its leaves are characteristically mitten-shaped, but often are three-lobed or oval. If you take one of the leaves and crush it between your

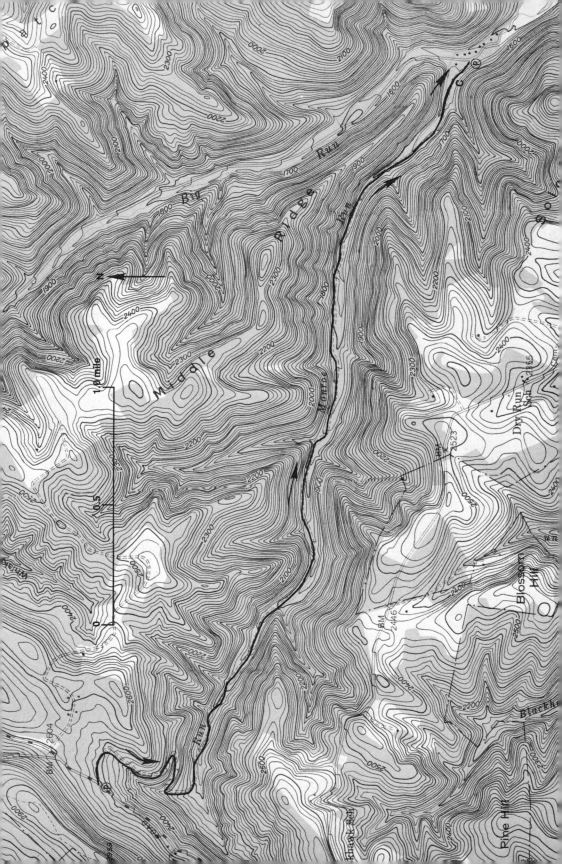

fingers, a rich, spicy, unforgettable fragrance is released.

The sassafras tree has an interesting place in American history. The native Indians showed the French and Spanish explorers how to extract oil of sassafras from the bark of the roots, claiming that this oil cured most ailments. The news of this wonder drug was carried back to Europe in the sixteenth century, and the demand for the oil and the price of sassafras soared, equalling those of some spices from the Orient. The settlers exported sassafras roots to Europe until the delusion that this oil was a cure-all quickly ended and the price of sassafras dropped. Oil of sassafras is still of some commercial value, however. It is used to scent soaps and perfumes as well as to mask the bad taste of medicines. It is also an ingredient of some root beers. Sassafras tea is a popular home-brew in some areas of the south.

During late July, golden chanterelles, a delicious mushroom can be found along this trail, side by side with poisonous mushrooms. Avoid picking mushrooms unless you know exactly what species you are picking. Some of them are deadly, even if consumed in small amounts.

The trail continues to descend, making a sharp right bend followed by a sharp left bend before reaching the headwaters of Monroe Run. Wild ginger and bristly sarsaparilla can be found along the borders of the trail. The trail follows the stream as it tumbles downhill through stands of hemlocks and thickets of rhododendron. Brook trout may be seen in the gently swirling pools at the bases of ledges and boulders. A campsite with a fire pit is passed at about one mile. The trail then crosses Monroe Run for the first of many times.

Here you have a choice of routes across the stream, either over a dilapidated bridge or through the cold water. Yellow mandarin, stinging nettles, Oswego tea, and black cohosh grow in the damp soils along the stream. Another bridge across the creek is encountered at 1.2 miles and another at 1.4 miles. The trail leads across a pair of bridges at 1.5 miles, and you cross twelve more in the next two miles. Many of the bridges are in bad repair, and it is often safer to ford the stream through the cold water than to risk falling through a rotten bridge.

You meet yellow blazes along the trail at 3.3 miles. No blazes are encountered until this point. The path fords the stream or one of its tributaries four more times before entering the campground at Big Run State Park. The end of the foot trail is marked by a pile of dirt across the path blocking vehicle access. To reach the vehicle you left near campsites #5 and 6, turn right and hike about a hundred feet to a fork in the road. Here turn left to come out of the woods between the campsites.

Harpers Ferry: Grant-Conway Trail

Distance: 7.2 miles
Time: 5 hours
Elevation change: 1,150 feet
Maps: USGS 7½' Harpers Ferry; Park maps
Highlights: Historical ruins, views

Harpers Ferry is probably best known for John Brown's ill-fated raid on the weapons arsenal there on October 16, 1859. Brown's twenty-two-man "army of liberation" attacked Harpers Ferry in order to mount an insurrection to free the slaves. They seized the armory and several other strategic points before the local people knew what was happening. Two days later, a contingent of marines led by Colonel Robert E. Lee and Lieutenant J. E. B. Stuart stormed the armory fire engine and guard house where Brown and his men were barricaded. Brown's insurrection was squelched. He was later found guilty of murder, treason, and conspiracy to create an insurrection, and was hanged in Charles Town on December 2, 1859.

John Brown's raid was the first of many acts of war to be centered on Harpers Ferry. Six days after the Civil War began, Virginia passed its ordinance of secession, and one day later Virginia militiamen occupied the town. The retreating federal garrison torched the arsenals before the militia arrived, thus preventing the South from capturing a great quantity of weapons.

The Confederate garrison at Harpers Ferry was commanded by none other than "Stonewall" Jackson. Jackson soon realized the strategic importance of Harpers Ferry to both North and South. He also realized how vulnerable Harpers Ferry was, sitting as it did in a low area surrounded by higher hills. He immediately sought to fortify the nearby hills.

The hike we describe takes you to the most important hillside military position for the security of Harpers Ferry: Maryland Heights. There, Stonewall Jackson's men built a wooden stockade called Fort Montgomery. The Confederate garrison later retreated to Winchester, destroying Fort Montgomery before leaving. To this day, no one knows the exact location of the fort.

Harpers Ferry was the scene of other clashes between North and South during the Civil War, and Maryland Heights was fortified by the occupants more than once. The ruins of some of these fortifications remain on Maryland Heights. The Grant-Conway Historical Trail was constructed by the National Park Service to allow visitors to Harpers Ferry National Historic Park an opportunity to view these ruins firsthand. The ruins have not been altered significantly, except by natural decay, since being abandoned soon after the Civil War. The hike not

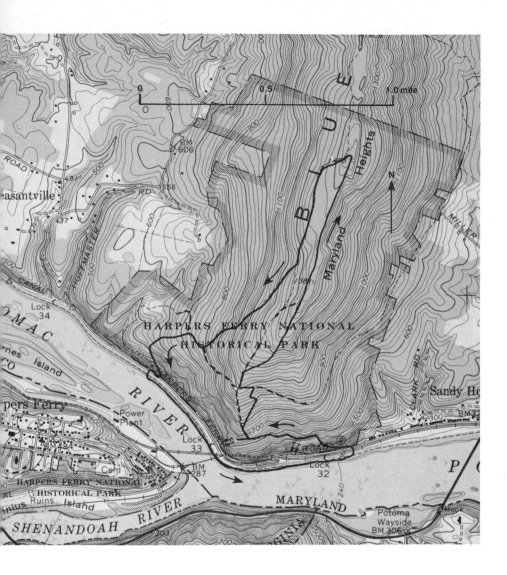

only tours historical remains, but also provides superb views of Harpers Ferry and the confluence of the Potomac and Shenandoah Rivers.

To reach Grant-Conway Trail from Harpers Ferry, follow Shenandoah Street and turn left on US 340 east, crossing the Shenandoah and Potomac Rivers into Maryland. Turn right at the first exit past the Potomac onto MD 180. Turn right af-ter 0.3 mile on Sandy Hook Road. The trailhead and a pullout for parking are 1.2 miles from this turnoff on the right side of the road.

The trail begins by climbing a set of stone stairs. Orange blazes mark the path. The trail is quite steep and rocky as it traverses the south flank of Maryland Heights. At 0.3 mile you reach an over-look where you can see the bridge over the Potomac. The forest shows signs of a recent burn at 0.5 mile.

The trail emerges onto the top of a high cliff at 0.8 mile. From here you can see Harpers Ferry, the two rivers, and the three states of Virginia, West Virginia, and Maryland. Behind Harpers Ferry is Bolivar Heights and to the left, across the Shenandoah, is Loudoun Heights. These were the other principal strategic military points, but because they were lower in elevation, the side that held Maryland Heights had the upper hand in battle.

The orange-blazed trail bends away from the cliffs to the right (north). Crossing back into the recent burn, the trail ascends steadily until it intersects with a little-used fire road. Turn left, and follow the road uphill until you meet with a small footpath leaving the road to the right at 1.5 miles. Follow this footpath, which is marked again with orange blazes.

At 1.7 miles you reach the site of "Six Gun Battery." Erected in October 1862, the battery was outfitted with six thirty-

View of Harpers Ferry from Maryland heights

pounder Parrott rifles and two twenty-four-pounder siege guns. With this artillery, the battery had a range of more than a mile and could challenge any attempts to capture Harpers Ferry or Loudoun Heights. At this point the trail forks, with orange blazes leading to the right, and blue blazes straight ahead. On the blue trail are signs of a military camp, with stone tent bases, chimneys, and ovens, in various states of disorder on the forest floor. You follow the orange trail to the right.

Just past the intersection, the remains of infantry trenches are supposed to exist, but they have fallen and been filled in to the point where they are barely recognizable as such. At 2.2 miles a "Powder Magazine" is marked by a sign. Now the spot resembles a hole in the ground, but such magazines were once covered by a heavy roof and six to ten feet of earth. They were used to store ammunition for the artillery. As you continue climbing, you come to a site labeled with a sign saying "100-Pounder Battery." The 100-pounder Parrott rifle mounted here weighed nearly five tons and fired projectiles weighing from seventy to one

hundred pounds. This was the most powerful weapon on Maryland Heights.

Looking at this site now, you may wonder what good a weapon like this would do in the middle of the forest. In fact, most of the ridge here was cleared to allow maximum visibility. Although this point seems isolated now, and protected by the forest, in the 1800s the gun here effectively commanded a large area.

From here, the Grant-Conway Trail follows the ridgetop to the top of Maryland Heights (elevation 1,448 feet). Beware of poison ivy bordering the trail through this stretch. At 2.9 miles you reach a survey marker indicating the location of the summit. Then you come to a partially built stone fort. The main fort, situated around the stone fort, was erected to prevent attacks from the north. Light guns and one thirty-pounder Parrott rifle were mounted on the north wall. Within the fort were more powder magazines.

At 3.0 miles a sign points toward a Naval Battery to the left, and a blue-blazed trail leads straight ahead. You turn left toward the Naval Battery, following orange blazes. After passing more powder magazines, the trail bends sharply left. The trail heads south again, now on the west side of the ridge. A large, flat area near the trail was the site of a military camp that had 1,000 resident Union soldiers at one time during the war.

The trail turns left onto an old military road leading down the side of the ridge beginning at 3.5 miles. At 4.4 miles this road intersects a dirt road coming in from the left. Turn right here, following the orange blazes downhill toward the Naval Battery. At 4.5 miles you turn left onto a footpath marked with orange blazes and another sign pointing to the Naval Battery. The site of the Naval Battery is a few yards down the trail.

In September 1862 this was the only permanent artillery site on Maryland Heights. In an important battle that month, Confederate forces captured the top of Maryland Heights, and this site could no longer be defended by the Union. At this turning point, Harpers Ferry fell to the Confederates. The importance of the strategic location of Maryland Heights is also illustrated by the fact that this defeat, of a 12,693-man garrison at Harpers Ferry, remains the second largest defeat of United States soldiers in our history.

When the Union soldiers regained control of Harpers Ferry after Robert E. Lee's defeat in Maryland, Major General George McClellan extensively fortified Maryland Heights to prevent a recurrence of such a disaster. Future attacks on Harpers Ferry were unsuccessful, largely because of the improved defenses on Maryland Heights.

From the Naval Battery the trail continues downhill, intersecting a jeep road at 5.2 miles. Turn left on the jeep road and you intersect Sandy Hook Road. You could follow Sandy Hook Road for about two miles back to your car to the left, but for a more scenic route, turn right on the paved road and follow it to a bridge crossing the C & O Canal at 5.4 miles. You meet the canal towpath on the far side of the bridge and turn left, paralleling the Potomac. A milepost (61) is reached at 5.8 miles. The towpath is a wide, tree-covered road here.

To recross the canal, watch for a small path traversing the canal bed at 7.0 miles. This path is unmarked, but it can be found just past a swift part of the river. A second landmark is a small, silver-colored building on the opposite side of the canal by a railroad track. After crossing the canal here, you can scramble up to the railroad track, cross the tracks, and find Sandy Hook Road beyond. The parking lot with your car is 0.2 mile to the left.

Chesapeake and Ohio Canal

Distance: 8.2 miles
Time: 5 hours
Elevation change: 120 feet
Maps: USGS 7½' Oldtown, Md-W.Va, Paw Paw, W.Va-Md;
    National Historical Park map
Highlights: Locks, Paw Paw tunnel, scenery along the canal
    and the Potomac River

George Washington had a dream that one day a navigable route would extend from the Atlantic Ocean to the Ohio River along the Potomac. He foresaw the need of a viable transportation system for growing commerce in the interior of the newly forming nation. Even with dredging and dams, the Potomac River proved to be too shallow and too rocky to be successfully navigated in all but two months out of the year. An alternative proposed in the early 1800s was the Chesapeake and Ohio Canal, also known as the C&O Canal. It was originally planned as a continuous waterway from Georgetown in the District of Columbia to the Ohio River near Pittsburgh, a distance of 360 miles.

The construction of the C&O Canal began on July 4, 1828, with President John Quincy Adams turning the first spade of dirt. In 1850, after years of problems caused by lack of supplies, lack of skilled labor, lack of cooperation from landowners for rights-of-way, and the difficult terrain, the C&O Canal Company dropped its plans to continue the unbuilt 180 miles through the mountains west of Cumberland to Pittsburgh.

The final C&O Canal went from Georgetown to Cumberland, Maryland. It was 184.5 miles long and cost $22 million to build. Seventy-four lift locks raised it from sea level at Georgetown to an elevation of 605 feet at Cumberland. Eleven stone aqueducts carried the canal over major Potomac tributaries. Seven dams supplied water for the canal. A number of waste weirs controlled the water level; hundreds of culverts carried roads and streams under the canal; and a 3,117-foot tunnel was carved to take it through a mountain. All in all, the building of the canal was a monumental task.

The canal operated until a flood destroyed it in 1924. Now the C&O Canal and towpath is preserved as the Chesapeake & Ohio Canal National Historical Park, which is part of the National Park Service. The towpath is perfect for hiking, biking, and camping in delightful surroundings where one can become immersed in the scenery and the history carved in the landscape.

The hike we describe along the C&O Canal is an 8.2 mile portion of the canal beginning north of Paw Paw, Maryland, and going south through the Paw Paw tunnel, then west to Town Creek. It is best done as a shuttle, leaving a car at each end. The end of the trail is located on the right side of MD 51 about 5.3 miles east of Oldtown. There is a small gravel road leaving MD 51 to the right and downhill into a grassy parking area. Leave one of your vehicles in this grassy area.

To scout out your return route, note that small dirt roads leave this spot going both right and left. The road to the left continues downhill into the woods where a gate prevents vehicle access. At this point a sign reads: "Green Ridge State Forest Circular Hiking Trail. Pennsylvania State Forest 19 miles. C&O Canal at lock 58, 21.4 miles. Total circle to this point, 39.4 miles. YCC project 1975-1980." This road intersects with the C&O towpath just beyond the sign.

To reach the trailhead, take MD 51 about 3.4 miles farther east to Thomas Road. Turn left on Thomas Road and drive 2.0 miles to Oldtown Road. Turn right on Oldtown Road and follow it for 2.8 miles to an intersection with Merten Avenue. Turn right onto Merten Avenue, which is a dirt road. Stay on Merten Avenue for 0.5 mile until you reach Outdoor Club Road, a poorly maintained dirt road leaving Merten Avenue to the right. Turn right and drive about 0.9 mile downhill to a wide spot on a curve in the road where you should park your car if your clearance is less than eight inches (you can keep driving if your vehicle is capable of clearing seven-inch bumps.)

If you park your car at this point, hike down the road for about 0.4 mile, where the road makes a sharp left bend and a metal bar gate prevents vehicle access. This is the trailhead. If you drive, park across from this gate in the wide spot often used as an unofficial campsite.

To reach the Canal towpath, cross the steel bar gate, and follow the track to the right of a large gravel pile. Signs tacked on some of the trees next to the metal bar across the road say U.S. Department of Interior Boundary Line, National Park Service. Park land begins as soon as you pass the gate. Just behind the gravel

pile, the road intersects with the C&O Canal towpath.

At the intersection with the towpath, turn right. The C&O towpath itself is a gravel or dirt track lined with grass. To the left is what appears to be a creek with slack water, which is what is left of the canal at this point.

The canal was once fifty to sixty feet wide at the level of the towpath, sloping to thirty to forty feet across at the bottom. Minimum depth was six feet of water. The locks were only fifteen feet wide and ninety-eight feet long, dimensions that restricted the size of the barges, which typically were fourteen and a half feet wide and ninety-two feet long with a draft of four and a half feet. Barges carrying up to 120 tons of cargo were drawn along the canal by teams of mules walking along the towpath. In the end, the canal was not an economic success, although it did provide a leisurely and important means of transporting coal, flour, grain, and lumber to Washington.

Within the first tenth of a mile, you cross a culvert going under the canal and the towpath. This culvert is one of many built to shunt small streams under the canal. Such streams would have wrought havoc with the water level in the canal, which had to be strictly controlled.

After you hike about 0.4 mile, milepost 154 appears on the left of the towpath. Soon after this milepost, you reach Sorrel Ridge Campsite. This campsite is equipped with garbage cans, latrines, picnic tables, and water. It is located in a very pretty spot next to a lock with the Potomac River close by on the other

side. All camping along the way is restricted to designated areas such as this.

At about 0.65 mile, the path crosses a wooden bridge where water from the canal seems to have been shunted into the river. Soon after this bridge you will encounter lift locks 63-1/3, 64-2/3, and 66 in rapid succession. Between locks, the water in the canal was at one continuous level. The locks connected the level of one segment of canal with another. The difference in heights between two adjacent sections of canal connected by a lift lock was from eight to ten feet. Each lock consisted of a short canal built of strong masonry with the bottom as low as that of the lower canal and the top as high as the upper canal. At each end of the lock was a strong, watertight gate through which the boats passed in and out.

When a barge was traveling from a lower to a higher canal section, the upper gate was closed and the water was allowed to reach the level of the lower canal in the lock. The lower gate was opened, the barge floated into the lock and the gate closed behind it. Water was then released into the lock from the upper canal so that when the lock was full, the water stood at the same level as in the upper canal. The upper gate was then opened and the barge floated on its merry way, eight to ten feet above the previous canal section's water level. It took from ten to fifteen minutes for a boat to pass through a lock. Only one barge could fit at a time, so this was much cause for delay.

After about 1.1 miles, the path splits

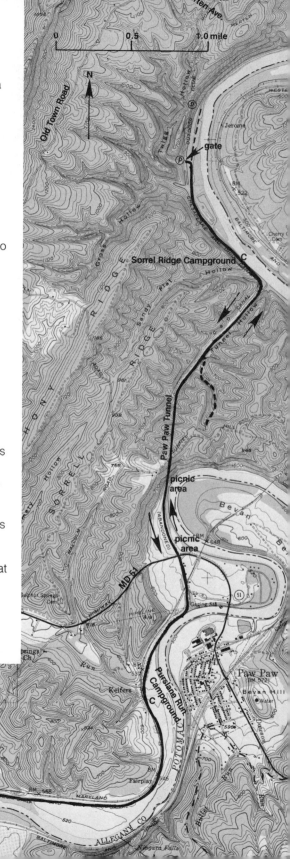

into three. Follow the middle route. The right track leads down into the canal, and the left track is part of an interpretive trail, but the middle track leads through the Paw Paw Tunnel past milepost 155. Here the trail is carved out of bedrock. A wooden boardwalk that lies against the right side of the sheer rock face of the canal leads into the side of the mountain.

This portion of the trail is not for people afraid of the dark. In fact, a flashlight would be handy even for those who are not. The tunnel is unlit, and it is nearly two-thirds of a mile long. In the damp dripping darkness, you can barely see the light at the other end. The tunnel is so narrow that only one barge could pass at a time. A narrow ledge along one wall served for the towpath where mules pulled the barges along. No steering was necessary in the narrow space, and the boats fit so snugly that they pushed the water up into a wall in front, making it hard for the mules to pull the load.

Just beyond the Paw Paw Tunnel is a picnic area with water, tables, trash cans, and latrines. This is a perfect place to stop and enjoy the awe-inspiring tunnel. Farther along, just beyond milepost 156 and 0.6 mile beyond the tunnel, are several well-worn paths to the left to a large picnic area with numerous tables and several old buildings. This picnic

area has vehicle access, as MD 51 crosses the towpath and canal at this point.

As you pass the picnic area on the left side of the towpath, you will hike underneath MD 51 and then beneath a Western Maryland Railroad Bridge. Purslane Run, another "hike-in" campsite, is found on the left side of the trail a bit before milepost 157. Beyond here on the left is an open field.

Although once it represented an awesome alteration of the natural landscape, the C&O Canal slowly is being reclaimed by nature. All along the route, the path leads through forests of silver maples, box elders, cottonwoods, apple trees, walnuts, elms, locusts, and huge sycamore trees. Every so often, small clumps of river birch can be seen growing on the floor of the canal. Wildlife is abundant along the trail. Frequently deer can be seen grazing along the side of the path in the distance, beaver signs are visible, families of ducks reside in the canal and in the river, and both painted and snapping turtles call the still canal waters home.

Three-quarters of a mile past milepost 161 and just beyond lift lock 67, turn right onto the access path that passes the sign for the Green Ridge State Forest Circular Hiking Trail. This short path is the one we described earlier; it leads to the grassy parking spot beside MD 51 where you left your vehicle.

Big Savage Hiking Trail

Distance: 8.6 miles
Time: 6 hours
Elevation change: 1,700 feet
Maps: USGS 7½' Bittinger, Barton; Maryland Forest and
   Park Services map
Highlight: View from lookout tower

Big Savage Hiking Trail is a 16.9–mile trail that follows a long, flat ridgetop in the Savage River State Forest in western Maryland. At 53,000 acres, the state forest is the largest in the region covered by this book and probably the most scenic in Maryland as well. The forest originally was established as part of the Monongahela National Forest, then deeded to the state in the mid-1950s. We describe the remotest stretch of Big Savage Hiking Trail, one lying adjacent to a "Wild Area" that is protected from human disturbance. At the time of this writing, this little-used stretch of trail was overgrown in a few spots with blackberries, so long pants are recommended.

To reach the state forest, take Exit 19 (Grantsville) off Interstate 48 and head north on MD 495. Turn right (east) at 0.7 mile onto US 40 (Alt.). You will reach New Germany Road 2.2 miles from this junction. Turn right (south) on New Germany Road toward New Germany State Park and Big Run State Park. At 5.8 miles from this intersection, a sign marks the point where New Germany Road enters Savage River State Forest. From the state forest border, drive 5.4 miles, then turn left on Big Run Road toward Big Run State Park. One mile from this

turnoff, Big Run Road becomes gravel. Five miles from the turnoff the gravel road intersects Savage River Road, which is paved. Turn right here. You reach a bridge over the Savage River below a dam 6.6 miles from the last intersection. Just beyond the bridge is a pullout next to the trailhead with a sign reading "Savage Mountain Hiking Trail" (really Big Savage Hiking Trail).

The trail initially follows a small, wooded logging road that parallels Savage River. White blazes mark the trail. You enter a clearing at 0.2 mile and then leave it on the right. The trail begins to climb steeply at this point. You can see the river and dam through the trees to your left as you ascend Savage Mountain. A fence along this stretch of trail prevents deer from falling into the spillway of the reservoir.

At 0.5 mile the trail begins a series of nine switchbacks. The Maryland Department of Natural Resources wisely urges hikers not to take short cuts between switchbacks. This would cause unnecessary erosion on the steep slope. As you ascend, the forest becomes increasingly dominated by oaks. At 0.9 mile a small

View toward Monroe Run

gap in the canopy has caused rapid proliferation of grapevines, which have overgrown the trail. Farther up the slope, the trail shows signs of disuse with healthy stands of blackberry, grasses, dogbriar, tree seedlings and, occasionally, nettles choking the path.

The trail gains the ridgetop at 1.3 miles, with more gradual uphill and downhill stretches past this point. A mile farther, the trail passes a wet, level area with an impressive stand of three- to four-foot tall interrupted ferns. Here, the trail crosses to the west side of the ridge.

At 4.1 miles the trail emerges onto High Rock Tower Road. To reach the high point of Big Savage Mountain, follow the gravel road uphill to the left for 0.2 mile. The summit elevation is 2,991 feet.

The road ends at a fire tower with a former ranger's cabin site nearby (only the fireplace remains). A rock outcrop near the cabin site offers superb views to the west toward Meadow Mountain and the steep drainages of Big Run, Monroe Run, Middle Fork, and Toms Spring Run (north to south), all headwaters of the Savage River. For a sweeping 360-degree vista, climb the fire tower. No camera can capture the exhilarating feeling of height and space from such a vantage point. You can't help but contemplate the great spans of time and the powerful geological forces that have shaped, and continue to shape, the Appalachian mountains and valleys.

To return to your vehicle, simply retrace your route.

Lost River State Park

Distance: 9.1 miles
Time: 6.5 hours
Elevation change: 1,800 feet
Maps: USGS 7½' Lost River; Park map
Highlights: Views, cabin

The land comprising what is now Lost River State Park belonged to the Lee family during the 1800s, when they used it as a summer home. The Lee family is a famous Virginia family whose members included Henry "Lighthorse Harry" Lee of Revolutionary War fame and Robert E. Lee, his son, of Civil War fame. Lee Cabin, a restored cottage and now a museum in the park, was a cottage belonging to "Lighthorse Harry."

This 3,712-acre park has cabins, swimming, horseback riding, picnicking, tennis, playgrounds, and game courts as well as hiking opportunities. It is located five miles west of Mathias. From the Broadway exit of I-81, take WV 259 west, then north, to Mathias, where you will see a sign for Lost River State Park pointing to the left on County Route 12. Turn left and follow CR 12 for four miles to the park entrance.

The trailhead is located on the right side of the park road 0.8 mile from the entrance. The trail itself is not marked, but it is the first "road" to the right past the park entrance (shown on the park map as the truck road to the fire tower). Parking is available there. The rocky jeep track is closed to vehicles.

The trail begins by crossing a bridge over Howard's Lick Run, and then ascends Big Ridge along a moderate slope through dry woods of pine, oak, and serviceberry. In a hairpin turn at 0.3 mile, Big Ridge Trail intersects from the right. You will return along this trail, but for now, continue to your left along the road to the fire tower until 0.8 mile where White Oak Trail crosses the road. Turn right onto White Oak Trail and follow the narrow foot- and horse path blazed in orange.

Wild iris blooms along the path in early May. These showy blue wildflowers were named iris after the Greek word for "rainbow." King Louis VII of France loved the flower so much that he chose it as a model for his emblem. The iris also was popular among American Indian medicine men. The underground stem was used as a poultice for sores and bruises, as well as a laxative. We do not recommend that you try it, however, for the iris is poisonous.

The path climbs through a switchback to traverse a flank of Big Ridge where the view opens to the southeast across the ridges. A sheltered rest bench to the right of the trail offers a perfect spot to

Big Ridge Lookout Tower

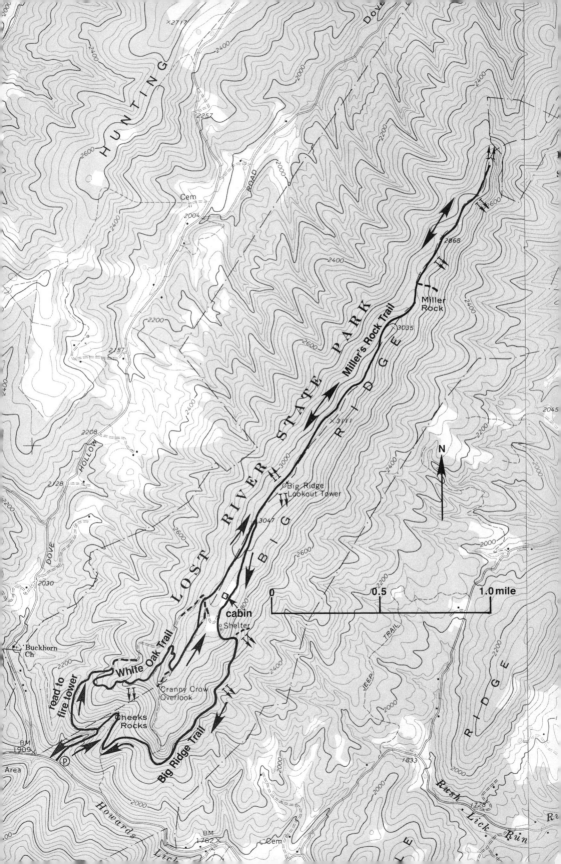

enjoy the view. The trail ascends to the north of this overlook through a series of switchbacks. Ignore all unblazed trails and stay on the main path. These trails are short cuts between switchbacks, and using them only hastens destructive erosion. Near the ridgetop, White Oak Trail enters a forest of short, shrubby pines. Views to the south through these pines can be enjoyed if you bushwhack to the right of the trail to the edge of a line of cliffs.

White Oak Trail intersects Miller's Rock Trail at 1.6 miles on the ridge crest. Here, a right turn will take you to Cranny Crow Overlook and Cheeks Rocks, while a left turn leads to Miller Rock by way of a fire tower. Turn left and follow the yellow-blazed Miller's Rock Trail north.

The southeast side of Big Ridge was burned in a forest fire in 1981. A grassy road leads off the yellow-blazed Miller's Rock Trail to the right to the top of the mountain into the burned area. If you take a short side trip along this road, you will be rewarded with a view down into a picnic area with a shelter — an eventual destination of the hike. You can also view the extent of the forest fire damage from here. This burned area is perfect for sighting the uncommon golden-winged warbler, which prefers a habitat with young deciduous growth.

Continue along Miller's Rock Trail about 0.3 mile, following the yellow blazes to an intersection with the road to the fire tower. About a hundred feet to the right of this intersection is a sign for Big Ridge. The elevation at the top is 3,206 feet.

Miller's Rock Trail continues straight across this intersection following a power line. Very near here and about 200 feet to the right of the trail is a huge oak tree with three children's graves at the base. The individual graves of these children, who died during a diptheria outbreak in 1915, are not obvious, but a semi-circle

of rocks at the tree base marks their presence.

The trail rejoins the road to the fire tower, which is grassy in this section. The fire tower and an attendant's cabin are on the right side of the road at 2.7 miles. This spot makes an ideal lunch spot for a day hike. After lunch in the grass beside the cabin, you can enjoy a climb to the top of the fire tower and capture a spectacular view of the surrounding countryside.

The wide jeep path continues north of the fire tower, staying about twenty to thirty vertical feet below the ridgetop on the west side skirting below a rock outcrop along the crest. Beyond this outcrop, the trail follows the summit again. Ignore all ancient roads intersecting the trail, and continue following the well-worn path marked with yellow blazes. The underbrush is thick with cherry seedlings. During early May when cherry flowers are at their peak, the air along this section of the trail is permeated with their pungent fragrance.

At a sharp curve in the track, the path begins a steep descent, levels for a short distance, then dips again. After the second dip, a road leaves to the right in the saddle, but the yellow-blazed path leads straight along the ridgetop. You are walking on the level in this section as the path begins to parallel the edge of Miller Rock cliffs on the right.

Miller Rock actually is a long line of cliffs with numerous views of the wide valley to the southeast. The views dramatize the meaning of ridge and valley province. In this province, long ridges neatly parallel one another, separated by long valleys. In contrast, the lands to the west of Lost River State Park are characteristically a disorganized jumble of hills and valleys.

The trail leads through a shrubby forest of blueberries and short oaks reaching only fifteen to twenty feet high. At 4.5

miles, the trail ends at the edge of Miller Rock at the tip of the ridge. From here you can view the countryside for a full 270 degrees.

To return, retrace your steps beyond the fire tower to the fork in the trail. Here, instead of retracing your way down the path beneath the power line to the graves, turn left and follow the unmaintained road. This grassy road wanders through the burned area and leads to a small log cabin in the clearing near the picnic area.

The mountain cabin, built in 1840 by William Tussing, is typical of cabins built during that period. A snake fence surrounds it, and an apple tree graces the front yard. Inside are two rooms on the ground floor and a sleeping loft above. A fireplace in the front room warmed the cabin.

Within sight of the cabin to the south is a picnic shelter and numerous picnic tables. A sign at the shelter points to a spring to the north on the mountainside. To the south of the shelter is an overlook offering another view of the burned area and the valley beyond to the south. The picnic site has outhouses, stone fireplaces, and a corral for horses.

The return route along Big Ridge Trail departs beside the corral to the south of the picnic area. Although the trail is blazed in yellow, the blazes are not obvious until about 300 yards from its beginning, where a red-blazed trail separates from Big Ridge Trail. From here, yellow blazes mark the way as the path descends through the burned area. The showy flowers of wild bleeding-heart flank the path from May to August.

To the left of the trail is a wide open view across the burned area into the valley below. To the right of the path is an impressive cliff topped with short scrubby pines. The trail circles the mountain, eventually leaving the burn and entering a chestnut oak forest to rejoin the road to the fire tower at 8.8 miles. Turn left on this road and retrace your steps to the trailhead and your vehicle.

50

North Fork Mountain Trail

Distance: 26.8 miles
Time: 2 to 3 days
Elevation change: 4,580 feet
Maps: USGS 7½′ Petersburg West, Hopeville, Upper Tract,
  Franklin, Circleville
Highlights: Views, wildflowers, cliffs

North Fork Mountain Trail ascends a high ridge just east of the well-known Seneca Rocks. By skirting a series of cliffs and smaller rock outcrops, the trail provides access to some of the most outstanding vistas in West Virginia. The full 26.8 miles can be hiked by setting up a shuttle with a car stationed at your destination. Rewarding day hikes are possible as well by starting at either end, hiking toward North Fork Mountain and returning the way you came.

The southern end of the trail is near a small turnout in the road where US 33 reaches its maximum elevation between Judy Gap and Franklin. The hike description begins at the northern terminus of the trail. The north end is reached by turning south from WV 28, 1.7 miles west of Cabins, onto FS 74. The Forest Service road is marked by signs on WV 28 pointing to "National Forest Recreation Area, Smoke Hole, 14 miles." The trailhead is 0.3 mile from WV 28 on the right side of FS 74. You will recognize it by a sign with a hiker painted on it and a small parking area large enough for three or four vehicles.

Double-check your supply of liquids before beginning the hike: North Fork Mountain Trail has virtually no water any-

where along its length, and it's a long, steep hike off the ridge to reach a source.

The blue-blazed trail (#501 on National Forest maps) begins by ascending through an open oak forest with thin, rocky soil. Burned stumps indicate that a forest fire has ravaged the area recently. A series of switchbacks makes the ascent of the ridge slower, but gentler.

As the trail ascends, pines become mixed with oaks and the trees become smaller. At 0.8 mile, the trail gains the crest of the ridge. Through the pines you begin to get views across the valley of the North Fork of the South Branch of the Potomac. The trail continues its ascent, with occasional steep spots, along the ridge.

At 1.8 miles a view opens to the northeast and you can see the town of Petersburg. At 1.9 miles you come to the first of many rock outcrops and cliffs providing superb views to the west. From here, the first high ridge to the west is the Allegheny Front, the easternmost escarpment of the Alleghenies.

East of that 4,000-foot ridge, the mountains occur in long ridges. The valleys parallel these ridges, only cutting across them infrequently at conspicuous gaps.

One such gap can be seen below you to the north where the North Fork of the South Branch of the Potomac has cut through the ridge you are climbing. Because of these distinct landforms, the area east of the escarpment, including North Fork Mountain, is called the "ridge and valley province."

At 2.7 miles the trail begins to level off, still following the ridgetop. At 3.1 and 3.5 miles, rock outcrops a few yards off the trail provide beautiful views to the south and west.

It is common to see ravens and turkey vultures from these outcrops. The vultures are especially majestic as they soar to great heights above the valley floor. In flight, their six-foot wingspans and penchant for riding the thermals are suggestive of the golden eagle. When perched, however, the vulture indeed resembles its namesake, the wild turkey. Despite its size and graceful flight, the vulture suffers an image problem stemming from the human prejudice against most animal species that make their living by consuming other dead animals. Although its reputation may be tarnished by this lifestyle, in fact the turkey vulture may thrive today in great numbers because of its reputation as a dirty scavenger.

Wild turkey populations, in contrast, are kept low by hunters, because of the bird's reputation as a delicacy on the table. And the golden eagle, a prized bird in almost anyone's mind, has been all but extirpated in the eastern United States because a minority of people fear that it will attack and kill livestock. It is understandable, yet rather ironic, that of the three bird species, the much-disparaged turkey vulture is the most successful.

At 3.5 and 3.7 miles, level areas near the trail provide ideal campsites. At 4.3 miles Landes Trail (#502) joins North Fork Mountain Trail from the left. Landes Trail provides another access route to the ridgetop from FS 74. For the next three

miles the path continues following the ridge, but now the trail is relatively flat and shaded by trees. At 7.8 miles Redman Run Trail (#507), another access from FS 74, merges from the left. Begin-

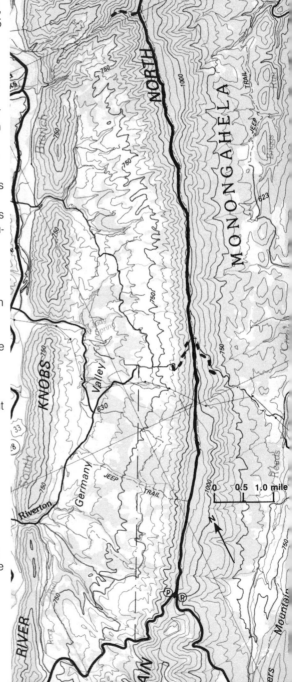

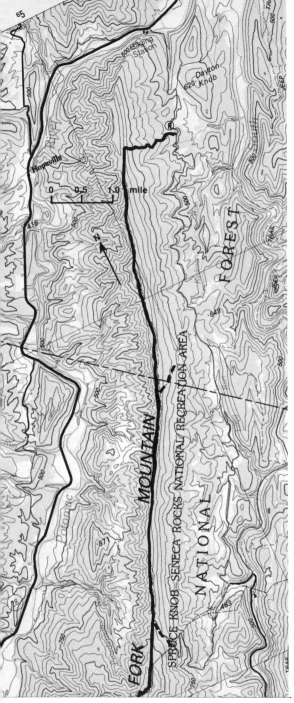

private land. At 9.3 miles the trail re-enters National Forest Land.

The trail alternately follows and dips below the ridge crest on the east side for the next few miles. At 9.6 and 9.8 miles the forest becomes glady, and fine views open to the east toward the Blue Ridge. At 10.5 miles an unblazed, overgrown trail turns left: stay to the right here, following blue blazes. At 12.3 miles, an overlook thirty yards west of the trail provides a view of a small sheep and cattle farm in the Powdermill Run drainage on the side of the ridge below you. In summer and fall you may see hay in the fields piled around a pole: old-fashioned haystacks.

At 13.4 miles, the trail intersects a gravel road that leads to a former fire tower site. At this junction a well-used campsite is available on the roadside. Follow the road uphill (straight ahead) toward the summit of North Fork Mountain (elevation 3,776 feet). The road crosses a gas and power line at 14.1 miles. From here you can see as far as Virginia's Blue Ridge Mountains and far to the south. Through a pair of switch-backs, the road eventually climbs to the summit at 14.9 miles near a radio antenna.

At 15.0 miles the road forks, and you take the left fork. At 15.5 miles you follow a small jeep road that veers left into the woods (the right fork leads to a micro-wave relay tower that can be seen about seventy-five yards ahead). At 15.9 miles, the jeep trail comes to a nice wooded tent site in the saddle between North Fork Mountain and High Knob (elevation just over 3,800 feet). Here, the jeep trail ends and the trail continues straight ahead.

At 16.0 miles the trail ascends to a high point on the ridge and crosses to the west side of the peak. The trail then passes High Knob on the west side of the peak at 16.2. At 17.3 and 17.4 miles,

ning at this junction the trail follows the edge of the National Forest boundary on

High cliffs on North Fork Mountain

rock outcrops to the right of the trail offer nice views of Roy Gap near Seneca Rocks. The valley between the ridge forming Seneca Rocks and North Fork Mountain is called Germany Valley. The well-kept small farms of this rugged region attest to the tenacity and character of the people who settled here and whose families continue to make their lives here.

At 18.1 miles, the trail descends steeply on the east side of the ridge. The ridge crest then descends to meet the trail at 18.4 miles. Although the path is somewhat overgrown by locust seedlings at 18.9 miles, you remain on top of the ridge. The trail descends again at 19.6 miles, then levels out within 0.2 mile.

A painted bearing tree at 20.3 miles marks the boundary of National Forest land and the trail is once again on private property. More views to the west are possible along this section of the trail. The trail becomes a jeep road at 21.7 miles, and at 22.0 miles you reach a junction with another jeep road.

The jeep road to the right leads to Germany Valley, while the road to the left goes to Reeds Creek. A tent site is available at this intersection. North Fork Mountain Trail takes you straight ahead toward US 33. At 22.7 and 22.9 miles, two abandoned jeep roads turn left off the trail. At 23.0 miles, the trail crosses a power line, opening nice views to the west.

As the trail approaches US 33, there are more campsites (at 25.7 and 26.1 miles) and excellent views. At 26.4 miles an old sign asking visitors to register is found on the side of the trail, but the register is gone. At 26.8 miles the trail emerges in a clearing adjacent to US 33 where your car is parked. Water may be found by following US 33 west for about 0.7 mile, where a small spring flows from the hillside on the right side of the road.

Guidebooks from Backcountry Publications

Written for people of all ages and experience, these popular and carefully prepared books feature detailed trail and tour directions, notes on points of interest and natural phenomena, maps and photographs.

Walks and Rambles Series

Walks and Rambles on The Delmarva Peninsula, by Jay Abercrombie $8.95
Walks and Rambles in Westchester (NY) and Fairfield (CT) Counties, by Kaye Anderson $7.95
Walks and Rambles in Rhode Island, by Ken Weber $8.95
25 Walks in the Dartmouth-Lake Sunapee Region, by Mary L. Kibling $4.95

Biking Series

25 Bicycle Tours in Maine, by Howard Stone $8.95
25 Bicycle Tours in Vermont, by John Freidin $7.95
25 Bicycle Tours in New Hampshire, by Tom and Susan Heavey $6.95
25 Bicycle Tours in the Finger Lakes, by Mark Roth and Sally Waters $6.95
25 Bicycle Tours in and around New York City, by Dan Carlinsky and David Heim $6.95
25 Bicycle Tours in Eastern Pennsylvania, by Dale Adams and Dale Speicher $6.95

Canoeing Series

Canoe Camping Vermont and New Hampshire Rivers, by Roioli Schweiker $6.95
Canoeing Central New York, by William P. Ehling $8.95
Canoeing Massachusetts, Rhode Island and Connecticut, by Ken Weber $7.95

Hiking Series

Discover the South Central Adirondacks, by Barbara McMartin $8.95
Discover the Adirondacks 2, by Barbara McMartin $7.95
50 Hikes in the Adirondacks, by Barbara McMartin $9.95
50 Hikes in Central New York, by William P. Ehling $8.95
50 Hikes in the Hudson Valley, by Barbara McMartin and Peter Kick $9.95
50 Hikes in Central Pennsylvania, by Tom Thwaites $9.95
50 Hikes in Eastern Pennsylvania, by Carolyn Hoffman $8.95
50 Hikes in Western Pennsylvania, by Tom Thwaites $8.95   •
50 Hikes in Maine, by John Gibson $8.95
50 Hikes in the White Mountains, by Daniel Doan $9.95
50 More Hikes in New Hampshire, by Daniel Doan $9.95
50 Hikes in Vermont, 3rd edition, revised by the Green Mountain Club $8.95
50 Hikes in Massachusetts, by John Brady and Brian White $9.95
50 Hikes in Connecticut, by Gerry and Sue Hardy $8.95
50 Hikes in West Virginia, by Ann and Jim McGraw $9.95

The above titles are available at bookstores and at certain sporting goods stores or may be ordered directly from the publisher. For complete descriptions of these and other guides, write: Backcountry Publications, P.O. Box 175, Woodstock, VT 05091.